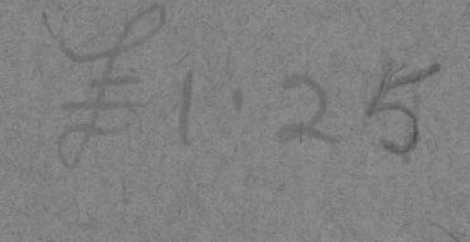
£1·25

D1346516

Our Goal Is Excellence

OTHER BOOKS BY DR. FISHER:

The Time Is Now
Second-hand Religion
Wake Up and Lift
Our Heritage and Our Hope
This Uncommitted Generation
Why I Am a Nazarene
Don't Park Here
It's Revival We Need
Evangelistic Moods, Methods, and Messages
You'll *Like* Being a Christian

OUR GOAL IS EXCELLENCE

A compilation of radio messages

by
C. WILLIAM FISHER

BEACON HILL PRESS OF KANSAS CITY
Kansas City, Missouri

First Printing, 1971

Printed in the
United States of America

Foreword

There have been few, if any, radio preachers better suited to their task than Dr. C. William Fisher. Gifted with a rich quality of voice, he speaks with careful diction and clear enunciation, packing into a six-minute sermon an hour of truth.

He has been the speaker on the "Showers of Blessing" radio broadcast for more than two years. From every section of North America and from many other world areas have come letters of appreciation for his strong, clear, and uncompromising ministry. Many thousands of copies of his sermons have been requested. The demand for some like "The Heart Is a Rebel," "Just How Great Is Our Society?" and "Come Easy, Go Easy" has been almost phenomenal.

I am pleased that 30 of these messages have been brought together in this book, *Our Goal Is Excellence*. They will bring blessing and strength to many.

—H. Dale Mitchell
Executive Director
Communications Commission
Church of the Nazarene

Preface

"Sermons were not meant to be read, as essays are," said a famous preacher. "The dominant factor in an essay is the *subject* to be elucidated, while the dominant factor in a sermon is the *object* to be attained."

This is especially true of the messages in this book, which were delivered with the prayerful hope that "verdicts" would ensue.

My "objective" has been to proclaim Christ in such a way that those who listen will not merely admire Him, but accept Him, and surrender to Him and follow Him in true discipleship.

That I have failed to lift up Jesus as fully as He should be lifted up, I am the first to admit. But it is a profound and thrilling challenge to keep trying.

To Dr. H. Dale Mitchell and all those involved in producing the radio program so that it can truly be "Showers of Blessing," my sincere thanks for their understanding and encouragement.

And my deepest gratitude to all those who have so graciously written saying, "Please send me a copy of . . ." Those opening words in so many letters, in fact, form the title of the first section of this book.

May the Holy Spirit, who alone can make the spoken word spiritually penetrating and productive, now make the written word effective in glorifying Christ, in whose name these messages were prepared and delivered.

—C. William Fisher

Contents

(Continued on next page)

1

"Please Send Me . . ."

Our Goal Is Excellence

***Covet earnestly the best gifts: and yet shew I unto you a more excellent way* (I Cor. 12:31).**

The waitress had just put the check on the table, face down, when I noticed those words on the back: "Our goal is excellence."

But shouldn't that be *everyone's* goal? I thought. Especially every Christian's? And more especially everyone who believes in holiness? For what is the life of holiness, after all, but a life of *spiritual* excellence, or a striving after it?

"Whoever I am or whatever I am doing," says John W. Gardner in his book on *Excellence,* "some kind of excellence is within my reach."

It is not in the reach of all, or even of many, to achieve excellence in sports, or in music, or in art, or in scholarship—or in any other field. But *anyone,* with the help of God's grace and power, can achieve excellence in the life of the spirit, for His help is available to all.

"The noblest search of today," said a president of the United States, "is the search for excellence. In every endeavor, there simply cannot be any lessening in this search." If we are searching for excellence in other areas of life, why not, then, a more intense search for excellence in spiritual living?

But that's just it: excellence is always expensive—whether in building a house, or a car, or a rocket, or a mousetrap, or a skyscraper, *or* in the building of a life. Excellence can always be bought, but it is never on sale. It can never be purchased at a discount house, for there are no markdowns on excellence in any endeavor of life.

A real pro, in any field, is one who is willing to pay whatever price is necessary for his best.

He is the baseball star who is willing to spend hours and days trying to improve his technique—even after his reputation is made.

He is the writer who revises his manuscript right up to the time of submission, trying to say it better—even after he has worldwide fame.

He is the musician who practices endlessly trying to sing it better or play it better—even after he has been proclaimed a genius.

He is the Christian who realizes that he doesn't "have it made" just because he has been to the altar once or twice, but continues to pray and work and improve and develop by keeping himself open to the fresh challenges of the Spirit—even after he's made a "decision" for Christ, or joined a church, or been saved and sanctified.

And what is the price for spiritual excellence?

Confession, consecration, constancy.

I confess my sins. I tell God that I am sorry for every evil thought, every evil act, every indulgence of evil habit, pleasure, or amusement. And He promises that if I "confess" my "sins, he is faithful and just to forgive" my "sins" (I John 1:9). So I believe His promise and trust His forgiving grace, and the work is done. My sins, even mine, are forgiven.

I then consecrate my *self* to Him. I surrender my will to His will. I say, "O God, take me and use me and do with me as You will. I am Yours, completely Yours." And in that moment of consecration and trust, the Altar does sanctify the gift and God cleanses the heart, cancels the inner contradiction, resolves the inner conflict, and frees me to do His will.

And now, in the power of His Spirit, I am able to move more surely toward maturity, constantly striving to exceed my previous best—in character, in service, in sacrifice. And isn't that the only true achievement, in any field: to constantly try to exceed one's previous best? "Forgetting those things which are behind," said Paul, "and reaching forth unto those things which are before, I press toward the mark for the prize" (Phil. 3:13-14). And the "prize" is not merely what we get; it is what we become.

Our goal, then, is not one trip to the altar, or even two. Our goal is not this "experience" or that. Our goal is not some rule or regulation or ordinance or ethic or position or prestige. Our goal is *excellence*—spiritual excellence; a certain style of life, a certain manner of living, a certain bigness of spirit, a certain point of view, a certain frame of reference, a certain set of priorities, a certain hierarchy of values—and above everything else, a certain love-relationship with Jesus Christ that results in an inner awareness of His presence, His power, His peace—and a continued acknowledgment that the very boundary of our existence is His will for our lives.

For Christ, and Christ alone, is both the *Goal* and the *Gateway* to that ultimate of spiritual excellence: Christlikeness. And who has ever fully, totally, reached that goal? "The most fatal thing to an ideal," said Schopenhauer, "is its realization." But through all of life, and through all of eternity, no one will ever quite realize that ideal or will ever quite reach that goal—but, oh, the joy and the thrill and the challenge of constantly trying!

And that continual striving, not in fear or frustration or in feverishness, but in peace and purity and in the power of His Spirit, is the life of holiness—the life of *spiritual* excellence.

"Our goal is excellence."

Won't you make it yours?

This Relevance Bit

***For I am not ashamed of the gospel of Christ: for it is the power of God unto salvation to every one that believeth* (Rom. 1:16).**

I don't know about you, but I am fed up to here with all the fancy, faddish talk about "relevance."

It has become the "magic" word—say it, and you win the prize.

Some "get-with-it" preachers, for instance, and some "swinging" churches, have become so desperate in their attempt to be "relevant" that they have desecrated the sanctuary with rock-and-roll dances and jazz combos and pornographic art shows and obscene plays. They have debased the pulpit with a so-called theology that has more in common with the Playboy "philosophy" and the *Daily Worker* than with the Bible and orthodoxy.

Those who are selling their souls and their churches for a mess of so-called "relevance," should listen carefully to Rabbi Arthur Hertzberg, who is also a professor at Columbia University.

"Religion as an ongoing force," he says, "cannot be saved by making it 'relevant.' People come to religion because they are possessed of an ultimate metaphysical hunger, and when this hunger is not satisfied, religion declines. Christians who are trying to revitalize religion by making it socially relevant should note the experience of Jews who started it a century ago. It doesn't work. The very moment clerics become more worldly the world goes to hell all the faster.

"The role of religion," the professor continues, "is not to gain acceptability in the secular world, but to expound the existence of God and man's obedience to a transcendental God."

Would that all professors, including those in church-related colleges and seminaries, believed that—especially those who, in the name of "relevance," ridicule and disparage the tremendous contribution of earlier Christians whose incredible devotion and sacrifice filled the reservoir of spiritual heritage that is now being frittered away by their descendants who mistake cleverness for commitment, and ridicule for relevance.

And students, also, should heed the rabbi's warning—especially those who are either too inexperienced to know or too prejudiced to see, that the spectrum of truth and the "whole counsel of God" is much wider than the selfish concerns of a few students who are up-tight about their own insecurities and compromises. These are the ones who take out their frustrations on, and brand as "irrelevant," anyone —preacher, professor, or parent—who does not spend his entire time discussing their own particular hang-ups.

I feel like saying with Jess Moody, "I want to stare right back into the faces of those who keep saying, 'Get relevant,' and say to them: Get reverent! When will you become reverent before the Scriptures? . . . When will you become reverent about the deity of Christ?"

What, after all, makes a church, or a preacher, relevant? Soft soap? Smooth public relations? "Exciting" social programs? Carrying placards in protest parades? Dances and dirty plays in the sanctuary?

Does a guitar in the place of an organ *really* make the church more relevant? Is a preacher carrying a sign in a parade really more relevant than one on his knees helping a sin-sick soul to Christ? Does it really make the church more relevant to lower its standards to the level of the unregenerate until it becomes easier to join the church than to join Kiwanis or Rotary? Or to dilute the gospel until it is indistinguishable from the political platform of Americans for Democratic Action? Are sit-ins and cook-outs really more relevant to the Church's redemptive mission than revivals?

No! The only thing that makes the Church relevant is its witness to the truth concerning the crucified and risen Lord. And the only thing that makes that witness *redemptive* is the power of the Holy Spirit.

It is still relevant to proclaim that "all have sinned, and come short of the glory of God" (Rom. 3:23). No amount of education or sophistication has changed that.

It is still relevant to warn a secularized, sex-crazed, hell-bound generation that, "Unless ye repent, ye shall all likewise perish" (Luke 13:3). No amount of money or missiles or moon-walks have changed that.

It is still relevant to remind all of the Church's "gravediggers" and "undertakers" that Jesus said, "I will build my church, and the gates of hell shall not prevail against it" (Matt. 16:18). There were those who one day thought the ark of God was falling, but it was not the ark that was falling at all; it was a swimming in their own heads.

The most relevant question in the world is still the question asked by the Philippian jailer: "Sirs, what must I do to be saved?" And the most relevant answer in the world is still, "Believe on the Lord Jesus Christ, and thou shalt be saved" (Acts 16:30-31). And that is true and relevant for individuals, and also for nations.

If the Vietnam war were over today, and the race problem settled tonight; if every man lived in a mansion and had a Ph.D.—there would still be a lost world to save and a great gospel to proclaim.

Talk about relevance! No one is more relevant than Christ, for He is the same "yesterday, and to day, and for ever." Men write books and title them "Beyond Barth," or "Beyond Freud," or "Beyond Bonhoeffer." But no one has ever written a book and titled it "Beyond Jesus," for Jesus Christ is the Ultimate—always up-to-date. In every age, He is the Eternal Contemporary.

Yes, by all means, let's be relevant. But may God forgive us if, in the name of relevance, we lose our *reverence* for everything we say we believe and stand for. Instead, may we find our *true* relevance in proclaiming fearlessly and urgently the gospel of Christ to a bewildered, alienated, and sinful world. For that gospel is not only relevant; it is *redemptive,* for it is still "the power of God unto salvation to every one that believeth."

You Can Go Home Again!

***And he arose and came to his father. But when he was yet a great way off, his father saw him, and had compassion, and ran, and fell on his neck, and kissed him* (Luke 15:20).**

Thomas Wolfe once wrote a book under the title *You Can't Go Home Again*. But there is another Book, a far more important and true one, that tells about a son who *did* go home again.

No wonder the story of the prodigal son still pulls at the sleeve and tugs at the heart of humanity! For one thing, Jesus knew how to tell a story. For another, He knew men—their hungers, their heartaches, their hopes. And He also knew His Father—His compassion, His patience, His love.

"The ultimate theme of this story," writes Helmut Thielicke, "is not the prodigal son, but the father who finds us." And thus it ever is in the unfolding drama of human ruin and recovery—whether of a prodigal son or a prodigal race—God has center stage, not as a despot or a tyrant, but as a "Father." And the great sweep of the dramatic action is but to reveal His character, and His character is revealed as love—forgiving love, restoring love, abiding love.

The prodigal's basic problem, you see, was that he insisted on living life on his own terms instead of his father's. And that, of course, is the problem of our world today. And *that* is the essence of sin in any age, in any society, and in any soul. The prodigal wanted his freedom, but when he got it he didn't know what to do with it.

Societies, and sons, have found that freedom is a good thing, if it is used properly. Freedom can lead to fulfillment, but it can also lead to frustration. Freedom can lead to happiness at home, but it can also lead to a hogpen in the far country. It can lead to heaven, but it can also lead to hell. Freedom, misused, always leads to a new slavery.

But the prodigal came to himself. That is, he faced up to reality. Sin's illusions were stripped from his eyes and he saw that riotous living was not real living after all and that the freedom of the far country was a fictitious freedom.

It is never enough, however, to merely become aware of the outlines of our hogpen, or to feel the hunger gnawing in our souls, or to see the rags and the filth of our condition. We must do something about it. We can't clean up the hogpen, perhaps, but we *can* climb out of it and head for home.

Too many modern prodigals, however, when they become aware of their hogpen, are saying, "I will arise and go to the bar." Or, "I will arise and go to my psychiatrist." Or, "I will arise and go to my lawyer." Or, "I will arise and go to my priest or preacher."

But the prodigal who has really known the "feel" of the far country says, "I will arise and go to my *father*." For when the heart is really sick and hungry, "there's no place like home." When a man, in any age, goes against God, life goes against *him*, and the only way back to life is to come back to God.

A modern prodigal, on meeting his father, might say, "It's been tough, Dad. I don't know what happened. I just became maladjusted somehow. You were so strict on me when I was a child, and I developed so many compulsions and neuroses. I'm not really responsible for my drunkeness, you know, or my gambling, or my debauchery. I'm just a sick man—so don't blame me; it isn't my fault."

But the prodigal, in any age, who is really sick of his sins says, "Father, I have *sinned* against heaven, and before you." No hiding behind his mother's skirts, or his father's restrictions, or even his elder brother's hostilities. But in an agony of remorse and conviction he sobs, "I have sinned." Those words, however, are hard to say. They puncture pride and wrench the soul. But there is no forgiveness for any man until that confession is made. God is never soft on sin. He is never flippant in His forgiveness. There is no cheap grace—for any prodigal.

But when that confession is made, the Father doesn't condemn. He doesn't reproach. He doesn't say, "It's good enough for you." No. The Father puts his arms around him and kisses him and forgives him.

The rags didn't repel the prodigal's father. The filth didn't inhibit him. Not even the smell of swine could keep the father from embracing his son. For this was the hour the father had been waiting for. The lost was found. His son had come home!

But even though the father had longed for this moment, he had to wait until the son *wanted* forgiveness. (Not even a prodigal can be *forced* out of the hogpen. He must *want* to get out.) But the son finally made the long pilgrimage from "Father, give me," to "Father, make me." And that pilgrimage led him to forgiveness and restoration and home.

Do you find yourself in the far country? Are you hungry and lonely and desolate and disillusioned? Then I bring you good news! You don't have to stay where you are. You can get up and go home!

And as you go, yes, even as you go, you will see your Father coming to meet you. You will feel the welcoming warmth of His outstretched hand and you will feel His forgiving kiss upon your brow. You will thrill to the ring being slipped on your finger and you will find yourself sitting again at Father's table—not as a slave or a hired hand, but as a *son*—a son back home. There you will enjoy the happiness and hospitality and love and unending joy of life with a loving, compassionate, and forgiving Father.

Yes, you *can* go home again. Hurry home, then, won't you? Your Father's waiting.

The Heart Is a Rebel

***Whosoever will save his life shall lose it: and whosoever will lose his life for my sake shall find it* (Matt. 16:25).**

In A. E. Hotchner's book about Ernest Hemingway, he describes in graphic detail the developing depression that led Hemingway to take his own life. A few weeks before the tragedy, Hotchner asked his friend why he was contemplating suicide and Hemingway replied, "Hotch, if I can't exist on my own terms, then existence is impossible. Do you understand? That is how I've lived, and that is how I *must* live—or not live."

A few weeks later, the world-famous author picked a gun from the gun rack in his home in Idaho, and in one blast destroyed that imaginative mind that had given to the world stories that will be enjoyed as long as books are read.

Not many, of course, rebel in such dramatic and tragic fashion. And yet God said long ago that "the heart is deceitful above all things, and desperately wicked." And the world is full of men and women today who, in one way or another, are in rebellion against life, against authority, against the inevitables, and against God. And that is the very essence of sin—the insistence on life on one's own terms, instead of God's.

But that rebellious attitude is not new. Lucifer fell from his exalted place in heaven because he insisted on life on his own terms. And from the beginning of human life on this planet, men have rebelled against God and insisted on life on their own terms. Thus has the world been filled with tragedy and heartache and hatred and war.

When will we learn that this is still God's world and that

there is only one way that will work in God's world and that is God's way? How many more Koreas and Vietnams will we have to suffer before we wake up to the fact that God's way is not only the best way, but that God's way is the *only* way that will really work? For every human life is programmed to be lived according to God's will, to the fulfillment of God's purposes. And if one insists on his own way, and superimposes his will on God's program, the answer never comes out right, and life is not what it was meant to be.

But men in their pride and arrogance have always believed they knew best, that they were self-sufficient, that they, as Hertz says, should be "in the driver's seat." They have felt that they should live their lives on their own terms and so they have stubbornly structured their lives, and their systems, on greed and ambition and lust and selfishness. And Communism, which extols man's ability to determine his own destiny by economic and material manipulation, is only the latest expression of life lived on man's terms instead of God's. However, a recent refugee from Communism, fleeing the atheism and materialism of her own country—herself, as Stalin's daughter, a child of tyranny—said on her arrival in America, "Existence is impossible without God in one's heart."

Existence is possible without God in the heart, but real *life* isn't. For Jesus said, "I have come that they might have life, and that they might have it more abundantly."

And abundant life is impossible without Christ in the heart. For He, and He alone, is able to lift life from the levels of mere biological or physical existence to the levels of moral and spiritual reality and fulfillment. And He does it when the heart ceases its rebellion and when the will is surrendered and when life is accepted on God's terms.

Think, for instance, of a very successful man on the west

coast who had made several million dollars and was, at 60, president or director of several companies. Despite his apparent success, life had somehow gone stale and flat. To be sure, he had money and a beautiful home and position and prestige, but none of these had brought happiness. He was bored, jaded, and sick of existence as he knew it.

He awakened early one Sunday morning, and as the emptiness and meaninglessness of his life enveloped him, he turned on the radio to get the news, thinking that if he could hear of other people's problems it would take his mind off his own. But instead of the news, he got a religious broadcast, and a choir was singing, "Jesus never fails."

His first impulse, he said, was to switch to another station. But he continued to listen and the words gripped his heart as the choir sang, "Heaven and earth may pass away, but Jesus never fails."

He paced back and forth in his living room, then finally stopped and said, "Well, I've tried everything else and it has failed me. If Jesus never fails, I will try Him." And he knelt by a chair, confessed his sins, and told God that he was sorry he had lived his life as though God didn't exist or didn't matter. In that moment of his repentance and faith, Christ came into his heart. For over 20 years now, and even in advancing age, that man has witnessed to the reality and joy of life lived on God's terms instead of his own.

Jim Elliot, the young missionary martyred by the Auca Indians in South America, expressed it beautifully when he said, "He is no fool who gives what he cannot keep to gain what he cannot lose."

But Jesus said it even more beautifully when He said, "Whosoever will save his life shall lose it: and whosoever will lose his life for my sake shall find it. For what is a man profited, if he shall gain the whole world, and lose his own soul?" (Matt. 16:25-26)

When anyone, however, is willing to quit insisting on

life on his own terms, and begins to lose his life for the sake of Christ and others, and accepts life on God's terms, he finds life—real, authentic, joyous, purposeful life.

But remember, the Bible and human experience testify that *that* kind and quality of life can be experienced and lived and enjoyed *only* on God's terms.

Come Easy, Go Easy

***And Naboth said to Ahab, The Lord forbid it me, that I should give the inheritance of my fathers unto thee* (I Kings 21:3).**

Perhaps you read recently of the young man with hippie tendencies who inherited several million dollars from his grandfather and immediately began giving it away with outlandish extravagance, announcing through the press and the late TV talk-shows that he would give away his entire fortune to as many as possible, and as quickly as possible.

The entire episode was another dramatic illustration of the old saying, "Shirt-sleeves to shirt-sleeves in three generations."

While the grandfather had worked hard and invested wisely to amass that fortune, the grandson was squandering it as though money was going out of style and there would never be another tomorrow.

But, as they say, "Come easy, go easy."

As incredibly wasteful as it was for a grandson to throw away a fortune that had taken years to accumulate, it is even more incredible and tragic to see a rich national or spiritual heritage, that took generations to build, drained away, eroded, frittered away by harebrained schemes, half-hearted commitments, and easy compromises—and, worst of all, by those entrusted to enrich the inheritance, not deplete it.

It is distressing and disgusting, for instance, to see a generation that never built *anything* tearing down everything others have built up. They burn flags they never protected, demolish buildings they never erected, destroy property they never bought, tear down schools they never paid taxes on, ridicule freedoms they never fought for, try to destroy a country they are unwilling to defend, and cry for a peace they are too soft to make and too lazy to keep.

Upon returning to Athens after an extended absence, Socrates would ask, "What kind of young men do you have now?"

I shudder to think what the Washingtons and the Lincolns and the Pershings and the MacArthurs and the thousands of men and women who paid freedom's price with their blood would say if they returned today and saw some of the smelly specimens on our campuses and in our streets burning draft cards, shouting obscenities, defying all authority, and making a shambles of our courts. What would they say about those who denounce the decencies, destroy the freedoms, and squander the heritage that it took generations to build?

But this principle of "Come easy, go easy" is especially tragic when applied in spiritual matters.

What would the Pauls and the Savonarolas and the Luthers and the Wesleys and the Bresees say if they could return and see some of the spindly specimens who wear their names and profess their faith and give lip service to their ideals, and yet allow the realities of a rich heritage that took centuries to build slip through their soft hands and hearts?

These traitors to the faith mouth doctrines they no longer believe and try to evoke emotions they no longer feel—and are passing on to their children a faith that is too weak to sustain even their own loyalties.

It was John Mott who said that "Jesus never hid a scar to win a disciple." And yet there are those today who have tried to hide the scars and mark down the price of entry into the Kingdom, until it is easier to get into some churches than it is to get into most clubs.

Few sights are more pathetic to see than a church that has squandered its heritage and lost sight of its mission and is trying to justify its existence by doing those things that almost any secular organization can do better.

There are far too many church members today who are trying to live on the momentum of their parents' convictions or their grandparents' faith. They have never paid the price for a firsthand faith, for firsthand convictions, for real commitments to any distinctive doctrine or standard. So when temptations come, or the lure of the expedient becomes too strong, they find it easy to fritter away a faith they never paid for, surrender convictions they never held, and squander a heritage that cost them nothing.

It is still true that you get what you pay for. And a faith that doesn't cost much isn't worth much, and it doesn't do much, and it won't last long.

If your faith cost you no more than signing a card, or joining a church, or making a new resolution, or turning over a new leaf, then don't expect it to be worth much when the winds blow and the rains descend and the floods rise and the dark hours come.

But if you are willing to pay the price of repentance and restitution and surrender and faith—all of which are costly—then you can begin to build a life-structure that will weather any storm, withstand any criticism, endure any sorrow, because you are building on a Rock—the Rock of Ages.

In a time of shortcuts and discount houses and marked-down prices, with so many voices proclaiming an easier way, a cheaper way, a more sophisticated way—how desperately we need to sing,

Must I be carried to the skies
On flow'ry beds of ease,
While others fought to win the prize
And sailed thro' bloody seas?

Sure I must fight if I would reign;
Increase my courage, Lord.
I'll bear the toil, endure the pain,
Supported by Thy Word.

May *that* be our song, and our commitment—remembering, as surely we must, that with faith, as with fortune, it is still "Come easy, go easy."

2

There Are Sermons in Songs

Is That All There Is?

***I have seen all the works that are done under the sun; and, behold, all is vanity and vexation of spirit* (Eccles. 1:14).**

There are sermons in songs, they say, and if that is true, there would surely be one in the currently popular song "Is *That* All There Is?"

After each recounting of a childhood pleasure or an adult enjoyment, there is the haunting question: "Is *that* all there is?"

But men and women have been asking that question for a long time now.

Solomon, for instance, asked it a thousand years before Christ. If pleasures and possessions could add up to the complete and fulfilled life, Solomon would have had it made. For he was wealthy enough to indulge every passion; powerful enough to be denied no imaginable pleasure. Yet he pronounced it all "vanity"—saying, "I have seen all that goes on in the world. . . . It is a vain, futile business" (Eccles. 1:14, Moffatt).

In other words, Solomon was asking, "Is *that* all there is?"

And there are millions today who share the same disillusionment and are asking the same question. For in our affluent society we have more things and fewer values, more money and less meaning, more power and less purpose than any generation in all history.

No wonder, then, that increasing numbers of people, young and old, look at it all in growing disappointment or disillusionment or disgust and say, "Is *that* all there is?"

J. Paul Getty was listed by *Fortune* magazine as one of the two wealthiest men in the world, worth almost a billion and a half dollars, yet he was quoted as saying, "I wonder what real achievement it is to make a lot of money."

What is he saying? Sitting in his English castle and surveying his oil fields, his art masterpieces, and his properties around the globe, he is saying, "Is *that* all there is?"

But it was a young Jew—and aren't Jews supposed to know about profit and loss?—who asked, "What shall it profit a man if he gains the whole world and loses his own soul?"

In other words, Jesus was saying that *any* man whose primary goal was to tear down barns to build bigger barns was forgetting that no barn can hold what the human heart really hungers for; and that no man can ever have enough of what he doesn't really need; and that no matter how big the barn, or farm, or bank account, or stock portfolio—in the end, He would have to say, "Is *that* all there is?"

But what about pleasures? Surely they will satisfy the heart's hungers and fulfill life's demands.

But do they?

Solomon didn't seem to think so. Listen to him as he says, "I got me servants and maidens . . . I gat me men singers and women singers, and the delights of the sons of men . . . And whatsoever mine eyes desired I kept not from them, I withheld not my heart from any joy . . . and, behold, all was vanity and vexation of spirit" (Eccles. 2:7-11). The eye is not satisfied with seeing, nor the ear filled with hearing" (Eccles. 1:8).

In other words, after draining the wells of every conceivable sensual pleasure, Solomon was still saying, "Is *that* all there is?"

And millions echo that wistful, haunting question today. Even though the opportunities for sensual satisfactions have never been greater, or the emphasis upon sexual pleasures more blatant and continuous and suggestive—with pornography filling the newsstands and nudity filling the films—yet, after seeing and hearing and experiencing it all, increasing numbers are asking, "Is *that* all there is?"

Judy Garland was one who continuously and increasingly asked that. Famous at 18 and a Hollywood star at 20, she was surrounded with the tinsel and the glamour and the almost unlimited opportunities for sensual pleasure provided in show business. But when she would stop long enough to ask, "Is *that* all there is?" she would realize the emptiness, the sordidness of life lived merely for pleasure. And so she would try suicide or liquor or narcotics to ease the disillusionment of that tortured emptiness.

But the good news of the gospel is that "*that*" is not all there is—for the Gettys or the Garlands or the Smiths or the Joneses—or for *you!*

Thank God!—in Christ there is an alternative to such futility. In His love there is a solution to such emptiness. And in His will there is an answer to all such disillusionment and discontent and disgust.

For God is still saying that "a man's life consisteth not

in the abundance of the things which he possesseth" (Luke 12:15). And Jesus is still saying, "I am come that they might have life, and that they might have it more abundantly" (John 10:10).

The heart of every man is hungry for *more* life, not less; and Christ is the continuing satisfaction of that hunger; for no matter how much life we enjoy, Christ has yet more to give. And His ability to give is limited only by our appetite for what He has to offer. So don't go through life, singing mournfully, "Is *that* all there is?"—when you have the opportunity to experience the quality and quantity of life found only in a profound and satisfying love-relationship with Christ that enables you to sing,

Take this world with all its pleasures;
Take them, take them, one and all.
Give me Christ, my blessed Saviour;
He is sweeter than them all.

Love Is Not a Sometime Thing

***I have loved thee with an everlasting love: therefore with lovingkindness have I drawn thee* (Jer. 31:3).**

While we are thinking about sermons in songs, what about the song a famous entertainer uses to close his weekly TV program: "Everybody Loves Somebody, Sometime"?

That about says it for much of our so-called human

love—a kind of love that is so temporary and spasmodic because it is based on physical attractiveness, which is so transient; or upon youth, which is so fleeting; or upon some romantic mood, which can evaporate so quickly.

A little boy questioned his mother as to what she had said to his daddy when they were married.

"Why I promised that I would always love him, and be kind to him."

Thinking that over a moment or two, the boy said, "Well, Mommie, you're not married all the time, are you?"

But real love is not a sometime thing. Real love is always forever. No man proposes to a girl by saying, "I will love you for 10 days." Or, "I promise to love you for 10 years." Or, "You can count on my loving you until you get wrinkled, or sick, or gray-headed, or fat." He would not only be turned down; he would probably be slapped—and shown the door.

For love that is terminal is not love—it may be lust, or eros, or sympathy, or kindness, but it is not love. For love's vocabulary is always "forever and forever."

No human love could be called an "everlasting" love, however, because human love has a beginning. But God's love has neither beginning nor ending. It didn't begin in time, and it won't end in eternity. Love that has no beginning has no ending. It is truly "everlasting." Only God's love is everlasting because only God is eternal; and since "God is love," His is an eternal or everlasting love—as He says in Jeremiah: "Yea, I have loved thee with an everlasting love" (Jer. 31:3).

This everlasting love is not ours because we deserve it, however. Who could possibly deserve a love like that? God's love for us does not depend on our worthiness, or our merit, or on what we've done or haven't done. It is simply the character of God to love, for "God is love."

And His love is unconditional. Our *enjoyment* of His

love is, of course, conditioned upon our willingness to meet the requirements for receiving and experiencing that love. But God loves us no matter who we are. Whether we're black or white or brown or yellow; whether we're a Ph.D. or a grade-school dropout; whether we're good or bad, handsome or ugly, sick or well, rich or poor—God loves us. He loved us yesterday; He loves us today; and He will love us tomorrow.

There is only one thing that can keep us from experiencing and enjoying God's love, and that is *sin*. As Isaiah said, "Behold, your iniquities have separated between you and your God" (Isa. 59:2).

But notice, even sin cannot separate us from the *love* of God; but it does deny us the experience and enjoyment of that love.

Sin does not destroy God's love; it frustrates God's love. God cannot do what He would like to do for the person who rejects His love. One may deny that love, or violate that love, or be untrue to that love, or reject that love, but that doesn't keep God from loving.

I can hide in a cave, but that doesn't stop the sun from shining. It continues to shine whether I laugh at it or throw rocks at it or hide from it. I may shut myself off from the sun and so experience coldness and darkness, but the sun keeps on shining whether I am meeting the conditions to enjoy its light and warmth or not. It is never the sun's fault if I am cold and in darkness.

And so it is with God's love. I may spurn God's love, or try to hide from God's love, or shake my little fist in the face of God's love, but God keeps right on loving. My response does not determine God's character, and His character is love. I can freely accept His love unto salvation, but I can just as freely reject His love unto damnation.

Sin will separate me from God, and my refusal of His love will prolong the separation. But, as Paul said, nothing can separate me from the love of God. For that love is everlasting.

A holy God would have to hate sin, of course. But God is not only holy; He is loving. And so, while God hates sin, He loves the sinner.

You, my friend, no matter what you've done, God loves you. And He loves you so much that He is willing to forgive you right now if you will tell Him you are sorry for your sins. You will not be lost because of what you've done; if you are lost, it will be because of what you have refused—your refusal to accept His forgiveness, His cleansing, His reconciling love.

I challenge you to meditate on this for five minutes a day for a week. Say it over and over; let it confront your consciousness and seep into your unconscious: "God loves me as I am—not as I'd like to be, or as I try to appear to be—*but just as I am.*"

Of course you may have thought about it already. If so, accept His forgiveness just now, and begin to enjoy the glorious provisions of His love in Christ.

Who Will Answer?

Call unto me, and I will answer thee, and shew thee great and mighty things, which thou knowest not **(Jer. 33:3).**

Another of today's popular songs, made famous by Ed Ames, states various problems that plague and plunder mankind in these troubled times and then dramatically asks the question: "Who will answer?"

The song merely expresses the increasing doubt of increasing numbers of people as to whether there really is anyone up there, or out there, to hear the anguished cry of troubled hearts living on the edge of the abyss. And if there *is* anyone to hear, does he care—and does he care enough to answer?

This mood was expressed by one who stood confronted by a seemingly indifferent universe and asked,

What is it like,
You say,
To find that God is deaf?
To stand on some sharp precipice and shriek and shout
And hear but the mocking echo of the soul's own doubt?

This question, however, has been around for a long time. Eliphaz, for instance, put the same cynical question to Job over 3,000 years ago. "Call now," he mocked, "if there be any that will answer thee; and to which of the saints wilt thou turn?"

But who, after all, *will* answer the cry of the guilt-ridden, sin-scarred, alienated millions, standing on the precipice, desperately needing forgiveness and acceptance and reconciliation?

Who *will* answer the prayer of those Christians who have come to the awareness of the deep conflict between their wills and God's and long for a oneness, a unity, an identification with God's will that knows no inner pollution, no inner contradiction, and whose cry is, with Paul's, "Who shall deliver me from the body of this death?"

Just who *will* answer when the body is being whittled away by cancer's scythe, or the heart is being pummelled by persistent pressures, or the mind is being torn by life's tragedies and injustices—and the cry wells up from deep within the soul: "Why . . . Why . . . Why?"

It was Neitsche who said that a person could put up with any "how" if he only knew the "why." But that's just it. When it is impossible to discover the "why," what then?

To all those who ask out of cynicism, or cry out of despair: "Who will answer?" I bring good news!

There *is* One who will answer. There *is* One who hears every human cry. There *is* One who understands and cares. There *is* One who is still big enough, and loving enough, to answer.

And that *One* is the eternal and omnipotent and personal and loving God. And that God, who lives in the eternal now, is still saying, as He did in Jeremiah's day, "Call unto me, and I will answer thee, and shew thee great and mighty things, which thou knowest not" (Jer. 33:3).

And the record proves that He *does* answer.

Faced with an unbelieving nation and the skepticism and scorn of 450 false prophets, Elijah prayed, "Answer me, O Lord, answer me, that this people may know that thou, O Lord, art God" (I Kings 18:37, RSV). And the record is that "the fire of the Lord fell, and consumed the burnt sacrifice, and the wood, and the stones, and the dust, and licked up the water that was in the trench" (I Kings 18:38). What an answer!

And what about those three young men who refused to bow down to any idol, even though ordered to do so by a king? Did God answer? His answer was so immediate and so adequate that they came out of the furnace unscathed and unsinged. And multitudes who have cried to God as the heat of *their* furnace increased have found that he not only heard their cry, but answered, and by the light of the flames they saw their Lord more clearly than they had ever seen Him before.

Think, will you, of the thousands who have said with

David, "This poor man cried, and the Lord heard him, and saved him out of all his troubles" (Ps. 34:6). And, "In the day when I cried thou answeredst me, and strengthenedst me with strength in my soul" (Ps. 138:3).

That is not to say, however, that God's answer is always the answer we would like to hear.

Even Jesus, communing with His Father, said, "If it be possible, let this cup pass from me." But He didn't stop there. He said, "Nevertheless not my will, but thine, be done." Oh, how difficult it is, at times, to get out that word "nevertheless"! But that is the secret, that is the only acceptable response—"Thy will be done." The Cross was a strange answer—all crosses are. But it was the redemptive answer humanity needed. And *your* cross can be redemptive if it is born in acquiescence and surrender and faith.

Paul didn't always get the answer he would have liked, for three times he asked God to remove the "thorn" in his flesh, but God's answer was, instead, "My grace is sufficient for thee."

In other words, God's answer is not always the one we would like to hear. Sometimes He says yes; sometimes He says no. But if we say "yes" to His "no," He will make the experience, even though it mean suffering or sorrow, redemptive in our lives—and in the lives of others.

Call to Him, then, out of whatever situation you find yourself, and He *will* answer, for He said, "Then shalt thou call, and the Lord shall answer; thou shalt cry, and he shall say, Here I am" (Isa. 58:9).

Yes, Mr. Ames, there *is* Someone to answer—and God's answer is not only best; it is the only adequate answer there is.

On a Clear Day

***I know a man in Christ who, fourteen years ago, had the experience of being caught up into the third Heaven* (II Cor. 12:2).**

Another song of our times that suggests a timeless truth is the one which says: "On a Clear Day You Can See Forever."

I don't know, of course, where the writer of that song got his inspiration, but it could have come from the Apostle Paul. For in the twelfth chapter of Second Corinthians, Paul describes one of those clear days in his life when it seemed that he could see forever. The vision of reality was so total and so overwhelming that forever afterwards he could point back to it as a spiritual "happening"—a happening of such insight and power that even after 14 years it was still fresh and vital, illuminating and inspiring the drab days of fog and low visibility.

And Paul certainly had his share of drab days. In fact, the memory of his clear day was projected against the background of those depressing days when he had been shipwrecked and beaten and robbed and overworked and persecuted and had suffered from hunger and cold and exposure.

Added to his personal discomfort was the depressing condition of his times—times, as he said, that were filled with "quarrelling and jealousy, angry tempers and personal rivalries, backbiting and gossip, arrogance and general disorder" (II Cor. 12:20, NEB).

Could there be a better description of our times than that?

But did Paul merely stand by wringing his hands over

the terrible days that were upon him, or dissipate his energies in diagnosing or denouncing them?

No. Into the very darkness of his condition and his times, Paul allowed the light and vision of the far horizons he had seen on his clear days to penetrate. And the illumination of that vision gave him inspiration in the difficult and distressing days.

What a challenge for the disheartening present in which we find ourselves!

How easy it is, in days like these, to get lost in the fog—or "smog" (for our fog is saturated with so many pollutants)! How easy it is to be depressed by the Vietnams, the racial tensions, the youth rebellions, the pot parties, the decline of decency, the erosion of faith, and all the other denials and deceits of a time when, as one says, "micro-skirts and mini-morals are marginal manifestations of a deepening decadence"!

But it is precisely in times like these that we need to do as Paul did: remember and rejoice in the insights and visions and challenges of our clear days—the days when God's presence was most real, His love most warm, His will most certain, His power most adequate. In those days we saw very clearly the redemptive relevance of the Church, and the potential for peace and freedom and greatness for our own country and for the world if only men would repent of their sins and allow Christ to become Lord and Master of all life.

There are those, apparently, who have never had clear days like that. But it isn't because there haven't been clear days. It is rather because their windows have been so fogged over by fuzzy thinking, or steamed up by hatreds and hostile attitudes, or so smeared and smudged by sinful acts that they couldn't see out.

It was a clear day to Paul, remember, not because it was a day of intellectual stimulation, or emotional excitement, or physical well-being; but it was a clear day because of *spiritual* vision and perception and reality.

Those groping to see should remember Dr. McCracken's statement that "it is impossible for anyone to be intellectually certain while morally unclean." In other words, if you want to see, get the dirt off the windows!

How tragic to see those in the *Church* who have never had a clear day in which they saw the real challenge, the real hope, and the real task of the Church.

"The most critical time in the life of any church," someone said, "is when the vision is being carried out by those who never saw it."

And there are many in the churches today, on all levels, who are increasingly frustrated and bored and disillusioned because they have never had a clear day of vision in which they saw the unique mission of the Church. As a result they have no standard of measurement for relevance, and no inspiration sufficient to carry them through these drab and difficult days when real renewal seems so remote.

And what shall we say of the distressing and deplorable sight of those who shout their defiance in the streets, and burn and bomb the schools and the cities, and do their violent and obscene best to tear down a nation and a society that have given more freedom and more abundance and more dignity to more people than any other civilization in all of history!

Not all of those who fill the streets and shout, "Pig," at policemen are Communists or hippies. Many of them have simply never in their lives had a clear day in which they saw the real beauty and beneficence of their country. Never have they seen the hope it holds out to countless millions around the world, nor what it could become if everyone would build instead of burn, lift instead of looking on in hatred or cynicism or contempt.

The times call for greatness, yes, but that can be

achieved only by those who allow God to clean the windows of their souls. Then they can experience those clear days in which they can see to the far horizons and envision the great sweep and scope of God's purposes. Thus they will be encouraged and energized, during the dull and depressing days, by that vision of a day when righteousness shall cover the earth "as the waters cover the sea."

You Haven't Heard the Half of It!

I have appeared unto thee for this purpose . . . to open their eyes, and to turn them from darkness to light, and from the power of Satan unto God, that they may receive forgiveness of sins, and inheritance among them which are sanctified **(Acts 26:16-18).**

In the final message of this brief series of sermons suggested by songs, we take the subject from the gospel song "The Half Has Never Yet Been Told."

Poets and songwriters and preachers have been trying for 2,000 years now to "tell it like it is"—they have tried to proclaim and portray Christ the way they have seen Him.

But after all these years, no poet has ever really plumbed the depths of the mystery of Jesus Christ as Son of God and Son of Man. No songwriter has ever fully described the sufficiency of His grace. No preacher has ever proclaimed the full scope and sweep of His redemption.

In my own experience, though I have been privileged to preach Christ all across America and around the world, never even one time have I felt that I had lifted Him up as He should be lifted up. Not once have I been satisfied with the way I proclaimed Christ.

For these many months now you have permitted me to come into your homes, or your cars, or your offices, or your apartments by way of radio, and I deeply appreciate the privilege—and wish that I might know each of you personally. But I must confess that not one time have I talked with you about Christ but what I have felt, Oh, if I could only picture Him as He *really* is—if I could only tell the story of His love as it should be told! If I could, surely every needy, hungry, sinful, frustrated, seeking soul would be glad to accept Him, to surrender to Him, and to begin to live in loving relationship with Him!

But when I've said what I can say about Christ, I have to stand on tiptoe and say, "Ah, but He's better than that. He's more wonderful than that. He's more loving than that. You simply have to *experience* Christ to know how wonderful He really is."

In fact, every sermon on Christ could conclude with the words, "But, friends, you haven't heard the half of it!"

For after 2,000 years of songs and sermons about Christ; after thousands of preachers—from Paul to Peale, from Savonarola to Sockman, from the greats of earlier centuries to the Grahams of the twentieth—after all of them have said what they could about Christ, it is still true that "the half has never yet been told."

Not only about the *person* of Christ, but about the *provision* of Christ. And of that, it can indeed be said, "You haven't heard the half of it."

Thousands of you, of course, have heard of God's ability and willingness to forgive your sins. And I, for one, thank God for a clear-cut, Bible-centered, repentance gospel—and for those sincere and faithful ministers in all churches who still fearlessly proclaim it.

You have heard of *pardon*, yes; but have you heard of *purity*—that God is not only able to pardon your sins, but that He is able and willing to purge your soul of its inner defilement?

You have heard of *repentance*—the confession of your sins and the forsaking of them as conditions for being born again. But have you heard of the privilege and necessity of surrender, of consecration, of totally yielding that new life of yours to God, so that He can cleanse you and fill you and use you in the manner and measure that will mean your deepest fulfillment—and His glory?

You have heard, of course, of being *saved*. But have you also heard that you can be *sanctified?*

If not, then you really haven't heard the half of it.

For God says, "This is the will of God, even your sanctification" (I Thess. 4:3). And Webster defines sanctification as "the act of God making one holy." But a far greater than Webster, the writer to the Hebrews, said, "Wherefore Jesus, also, that he might sanctify the people with his own blood, suffered without the gate" (Heb. 13:12).

And Jesus himself, in His high-priestly prayer for His own disciples, said, "I pray not for the world, but for them which thou hast given me; for they are thine. Sanctify them" (John 17:9, 17). These men had already been following Him for three years—and yet He prayed that they would be sanctified.

And were they?

According to God's Word, that prayer was answered for those disciples on the Day of Pentecost. And from that day onward, Peter testified that their hearts were "purified" on that day and in that experience.

But other disciples, from Peter's day to this day, have also testified to the reality—not only of God's saving grace, but to His sanctifying power; not only to forgiveness through personal faith in Christ, but to cleansing through the purifying power of His blood.

"Tell it like it is," you say? But that's impossible! No one could ever fully describe the glory, the mystery, the infinite and sacrificial love that made such redemption, such reconciliation, such restoration possible.

But Christians around the world will keep on *trying* to tell as much of it as they have seen and experienced, knowing full well that no one could ever tell even the half of it.

3

For Holy Days and Holidays

But Just Wait till Next Year!

(New Year's Day)

Forgetting those things which are behind, and reaching forth unto those things which are before, I press toward the mark for the prize of the high calling of God in Christ Jesus **(Phil. 3:13-14).**

How many times have you heard athletes, after losing a game or a tournament—or businessmen after a bad year—or students after a year of poor grades—say, "But just wait till next year!" Meaning, of course, that next year will most certainly be better.

It is a good thing, once in a while—and why not at the beginning of a new year?—to have a "summit conference" with our best selves and to resolve that we will try harder. "Avis" says it the year round—surely we could say it at the beginning of a new year.

There are those, of course, who ridicule new-year resolutions. But *any* man should be encouraged who keeps trying, who keeps resolving—no matter how long or how briefly the resolutions are kept. For no movement in the right direction is ever lost. It was James Russell Lowell who said:

Greatly begin! Though thou have time
For but a line, be that sublime—
Not failure, but low aim is crime.

And it was Charles Lamb who said that "the person is either very bad or very ignorant who does not make a good resolution on New Year's Day."

What about starting, then, with one of these?

● I resolve to be a better man, a more thoughtful husband, a more understanding father—even if I can't stand that long hair and those sloppy clothes and that loud music. I'll try—I'll *really* try, this year, to understand.

● I resolve to be a better woman—a more attentive wife, a more compassionate and loving mother, and a more charitable neighbor and friend.

● I resolve to be a more thoughtful and obedient young person. I will try to be a little more human in my home, realizing that my parents are people, too, with feelings, and problems, and hopes.

● I resolve to be a better citizen, and at whatever cost I will not be guilty of the sin of silence when right is being ridiculed and wrong is being loudly proclaimed. If violence erupts, I will make sure that I am part of the answer, and *not* part of the problem.

● I resolve to be a better Christian, not only in more faithful attendance at church and in the support of its ministry and outreach, but in my daily devotions and witnessing. I will sincerely strive to come more and more to the "measure of the fullness of the stature of Christ."

Speaking of resolutions, did you read the story of the girl who, as she was putting up a new calender, was overheard to exclaim, "Oh, this is going to be a *beautiful* year"? When she was asked how she could be so sure, and especially since a year was a long time, she said, "Well, a day isn't a long time, and a year is only a number of days, and I am going to see to it that every single one of these 365 days gets at least one beautiful thing in it."

But of course not even *one* day of the coming year will be beautiful and fulfilling if we insist on dragging last year's failures and mistakes and sins along with us.

It was Paul who gave us the secret of fresh beginnings when he said, "Forgetting those things which are behind, and reaching forth unto those things which are before, I press toward the mark for the prize of the high calling of God in Christ Jesus" (Phil. 3:13-14).

When we have confessed to God our failures and our shortcomings and our petty attitudes and our resentful spirit and our short temper and our sharp tongue and our missed opportunities, then we can trust God to forgive them all—and He will! For He said, "If we confess our sins, he is faithful and just to forgive us our sins, and to cleanse us from all unrighteousness" (I John 1:9).

What a way to start the new year! Pardoned, forgiven, reconciled, with the slate wiped clean and the deep exhilaration of a new beginning!

No wonder that Christians don't need all the noise and liquor of a New Year's Eve party to drown out the memory of the mistakes and failures and sins of the past year. They believe those defeats are all covered by the blood of Christ and so they can face the new year, not in a guilt-ridden, alcoholic haze, but in the clear-eyed, clean-souled soberness of sons of God.

It is wonderful, of course, to have the past forgiven and under the Blood, but if the new resolutions are to be kept, if the new year is to hold victories instead of defeats, we must have outside help—we must have the help that comes only from God.

And the good news is that He has promised that help. For He said to all those who love Him and obey Him, "You will receive power when the Holy Spirit comes upon you; and you will bear witness for me . . . to the ends of the earth" (Acts 1:8, NEB).

With such a promise and such a provision at our disposal, let us then cast a grateful glance at the year just slipping by, and face the future with faith grounded in the Word and dependability of God. No matter the setbacks of last year, no matter the disappointments or defeats, we say with optimism and assurance, *"Just wait till next year!"*

And I, for one, can hardly wait to get into it! For I want it to be for me, and for you, and for Christ's sake, the very best and most fruitful year thus far.

Mission Accomplished!

(Easter)

This is a faithful saying, and worthy of all acceptation, that Christ Jesus came into the world to save sinners **(I Tim. 1:15).**
It is finished **(John 19:30).**
Wherefore God also hath highly exalted him **(Phil. 2:9).**

After the splashdown of "Apollo 11," the spaceship used in that historic mission that landed the first man on the moon, the men at Houston's Mission Control, 4,000 miles away, flashed on a screen John F. Kennedy's 1961 pledge that the United States would land a man on the moon "before this decade is out."

Nearby, on a smaller screen, was the immensely proud statement: "Task accomplished . . . July, 1969."

Millions of people around the world listened or watched with suspenseful fascination the progress of that flight and the incredible feat of a man setting foot on another heavenly body and then safely returning to earth. No wonder millions cheered at the successful conclusion of that mission, for it was, as Neil Armstrong said, "a giant leap for mankind."

At this Easter time, our thoughts turn to another "mission"—the greatest, most daring, most profound, and most meaningful mission ever undertaken. It was the mission of Jesus Christ to a lost world—not merely to set foot on it, or to walk on it, or to explore it, but to *redeem* it!

All the previous history of God's dealings with men, all the immense planning of an omnipotent and loving God to provide redemption for a sinning race, all the events in the life of Jesus—His miraculous birth, His miracles, His ministry, His death and resurrection—came into focus in this momentous mission of redeeming lost humanity.

"For the Son of man is come to seek and to save that which was lost," is the way Luke defines that mission (Luke 19:10).

And from the moment Jesus left heaven's glories, the hosts of heaven and of hell watched the drama of that divine mission unfold—from the touchdown at Bethlehem . . . to the preparation at Nazareth . . . to the gathering storm of opposition to His message and ministry . . . to the growing suspense of Passion Week that finally erupted in that awful, universe-shaking hour when God's own Son was crucified on a cross.

And when at last Jesus uttered the cry, "It is finished," the soldiers and bloodthirsty rabble around the Cross thought it was but the end of another wasted life. But those in heaven and in hell knew that those words announced the accomplishment of the greatest mission in history—the mission of Christ to redeem a fallen race. At last the power of sin was broken, and victory over Satan was assured. Christ, in obedience to the demands of divine love, had accomplished His mission, had fulfilled His task, and had done what He set out from heaven to do!

What a mission! And what a victory!

For in that moment on Calvary

. . . the deed was done
Which shook the earth and veiled the sun.

For Satan had unleashed his worst, and God had revealed His best. Christ, with arms stretched out on a cross, had brought God and men together in a reconciliation which had been in the heart of God since man's first disobedience.

At the successful conclusion of another "Apollo" mission to the moon, President Nixon, as commander in chief, honored the three astronauts, who were navy commanders, by raising them to the rank of captain.

With the fulfillment of Christ's redemptive mission to the earth, however, the eternal God gave honor and glory to His Son, Jesus Christ, by raising Him from the dead.

"For this Jesus hath God raised up," proclaimed Peter on the Day of Pentecost, "whereof we all are witnesses" (Acts 2:32).

"If the New Testament makes anything clear," writes Leonard Griffith, "it is this . . . The Resurrection of Christ was God's verdict upon His Son's perfect obedience. . . . Men showed what they thought of Jesus by crucifying Him; God showed what He thought of Jesus by raising Him from the dead."

This Easter, then, as Christians have for over 1,900 years, we celebrate that Resurrection. We glory in the successful accomplishment of that redemptive mission God set for His Son. We lift our voices in praise for the victory forever assured by His death and resurrection.

By radio, by television, from thousands of pulpits, in songs sung by millions around the world, the glorious announcement will go out today: "He is risen! Christ is risen!"

And in many thousands of hearts there will be the answering response, "Yes, He is risen indeed! I *know* He is a living Christ—for He lives within my heart!"

And Easter *is* an announcement. It is not an argument; it is not a theological discussion; it is not a beautiful but irrelevant sentiment; it is not cards or eggs or Easter bunnies.

It is an *announcement*—the announcement that Christ's redemptive mission to the world has been accomplished and that God has sealed that stupendous victory with the resurrection of His Son from the grave. It proclaims that from henceforth His followers have the privilege of entering into the provisions of that victory, and have the responsibility to proclaim it to the farthest reaches of the earth.

"A Christian," someone said recently, "is one who remembers two things: the death and the resurrection of Jesus Christ."

On this glad Easter, then, let us not only remember; let us *rejoice*—as we celebrate His victorious death . . . His empty tomb . . . and *a risen Christ!*

Tell Her Now!

(Mother's Day)

Favour is deceitful, and beauty is vain: but a woman that feareth the Lord, she shall be praised **(Prov. 31:30).**

"One of the things every minister dreads," said one high church official, "is preaching a Mother's Day sermon."

But I honestly don't know what he means by that, for I am grateful for this day that is set aside to do special honor to our mothers, even though it does nothing more than to remind us that whatever words of gratitude and love we wish to say, we should say them *now*—while our mothers are still here to enjoy them and be encouraged by them—even though, as one writer suggests, some women themselves would just as soon forget the whole thing.

This is not to say, of course, that all mothers are worthy of honor and praise. Dr. George W. Crane tells in one of his columns about a six-year-old boy who answered the doorbell one day and there saw two policemen.

"Where's your mother?" they asked.

"She's out stealing," the boy casually replied.

"Many mothers think they are good," observes Dr. Crane, "when they actually are only second-raters.

"For example," he asked in his syndicated column, "how many of you mothers smoke? Yet you know this is medically unwise and economically wasteful. How many mothers indulge in wanton slang and even profanity before their children? How many women drink liquor at home? Or sneak out to a neighboring tavern?"

Then Dr. Crane (who is an M.D. as well as a Ph.D.) mentions some characteristics of good mothers.

"Good mothers," he says, "read Bible stories to their youngsters; and good mothers not only prepare their children for Sunday School but actually take them there. Good mothers are liberal with compliments. But they also administer reproof and spankings when indicated."

Perhaps this is another reason I am grateful for Mother's Day—because by all those standards, and more, my mother was a good mother. Oh, she was never listed among the best dressed in the nation or in the state or in our hometown, or even on our block, but she did dress with Christian modesty. She never won an "Oscar"—she wouldn't have even known what that stood for—but she acted in the home as a Christian mother should. She never sang at the Met, but when she sang at church or at home she sounded like she meant it—and people were blest. She was no good at all as a public speaker; in fact, she believed in talking softly—and carrying a big stick—well, at least a switch! She couldn't possibly have held her own in any group discussing current fashions or fads or books or ideas, but she was able to maintain an atmosphere in the home in which it was easy to talk about God and the things that really matter.

It is Dr. Louis Evans who tells of the two young collegians who had heard a famous skeptic give a lecture which was highly critical of the Christian faith. Coming out of the auditorium, one of the young men said to the other, "Well, I guess he knocked the props out from under Christianity that time, didn't he?" "Oh, no," said the other. "He has not explained my mother's life, and until he explains my mother's life I will stay by my mother's God."

And that's where I still take my stand—by my mother's God. For I heard her sing many times, "He never has failed me yet"—and He not only didn't fail her in life; He didn't fail her in death.

Like so many of us, I suppose, I failed to express my love and appreciation as often as I should. But I am grateful for the times I did remember, and for the fact that a few months before her death I wrote her a long letter trying to express my love to her and my appreciation for all she was and all she had done. I still treasure her reply to that letter.

This Mother's Day, then, won't you phone or wire or write or go to see your mother and try to tell her how much you love her? Tell her *now*—don't just wish you had after she's gone. Or if you want to say it with flowers, surely you won't be like the man who ordered only two roses—explaining to the florist that he was a man of few words. You ought to make it at least three—one for each of those magic words: "I love you."

President McKinley was one of those who not only loved and appreciated his mother, but who told her so every day. Even after he became a congressman and then governor of Ohio and then president of the United States, on those days he couldn't see his mother, McKinley would either write or wire or call her.

And when he was informed that his mother was very ill and that if he wanted to see her he had better go quickly, the President replied, as he made ready to go, "Tell Mother I'll be there."

It was Charles Fillmore who, after McKinley's death, took those words and wrote a song with them—a song that *can* be used to express nothing more than cheap sentiment, but which can also be used to encourage men and women and boys and girls to get right with their mothers' God.

Tell her now, won't you? Don't wait for an angel to do it—*you* tell her now. Tell your mother that you love her, but also tell her that you will pay whatever price you have to pay to meet her in heaven.

Unemployed Saints

(Labor Day)

***For we are labourers together with God* (I Cor. 3:9).**

The U.S. Labor Department released figures not long ago which revealed that employment in the United States was at an all-time high, with over 80 million people with jobs.

But even with that unprecedented figure, there were, at the time of the report, still over 3 million unemployed—most of them unskilled laborers, plus the hard-core unemployable.

There is one significant employment statistic that the Labor Department doesn't supply, however, and that is the number of "unemployed saints" in the churches. We wouldn't expect that figure to be listed in official government reports, I suppose, yet the number of unemployed saints is a most disturbing problem.

The word "saints" is used here in the sense in which the Apostle Paul used it—meaning *all* Christian believers. And the word "unemployed" refers to those church members who are idle, inactive, or uncommitted to the real task of the Church, which is a *redemptive* task.

"The real hindreance to the church today," said Dr. James Stewart, "is not the increased secularism on the outside of the church; it is the decreased Christianity on the inside of the church."

And that "decreased Christianity" reveals itself in every area of commitment and involvement in the redemptive task of the Church.

In financial surveys, for instance, it is revealed that 80

percent of the financial load of the churches is usually carried by 20 percent of the membership.

One churchman said recently that one-half of the church members of America could die overnight and it wouldn't affect the work of the church or its outreach.

There are very few unemployed saints, however, when it comes to social activities. The number of suppers and showers promoted by the church caused one to observe that many church members are changing the song "When the Roll Is Called Up Yonder, I'll Be There," to "When the *Rolls* Are *Served* Up Yonder, I'll Be There."

In fact, in most churches today, parties outnumber prayer meetings, organizers are more prevalent than agonizers, and social activities take precedence over spiritual concerns.

Is it any wonder that increasing numbers of concerned people within the Church are becoming disillusioned, and increasing thousands outside the Church are becoming disgusted—as was revealed in a recent *Ladies Home Journal* survey, published under the title "You Can't Find God in Church Anymore."

Could there be any greater tragedy than the sight of so many unemployed saints—so many idle and unconcerned and complacent and dry-eyed church members—in a time of such challenge and conflict? So many areas of life—national and personal—desperately need the corrective that only a vital, relevant, and redemptive church could give.

There are enough church members in America to be a vital and corrective influence in the decisions made by politicians—from the courthouse to the White House—if the church members would get on their knees and *pray* for their political leaders, instead of standing idly by criticizing or bemoaning conditions.

There are enough church members in America to put an end to the pornographic filth spewing out of diseased and perverted minds onto the newsstands and into homes—*if* the church members would quit buying the smutty stuff and would rise up in righteous wrath and demand a cleanup.

There are enough church members in America to reduce or remove the tensions and hatred being generated between races and classes—on the campuses and elsewhere—if the church members would quit their hypocrisies and begin to live by the principles of Christian love and start practicing what they preach and profess.

There are enough church members in America to wipe violence and perverted sex off the screens—in theaters and on TV—if church members would quit attending the filthy shows and object strenuously to the companies which sponsor the lewd and lascivious programs on television.

In other words, every moral and spiritual problem that we have—the erosion of moral standards and the denial of spiritual priorities that are bringing us to the brink of degeneracy and destruction—could be solved if the church members who are standing idly by would become concerned and involved. Instead of *playing* church and patting each other on the back in their religious clubs while their families and their nation and their world go to hell, if all the church members would fall on their knees and get right with God, God could use them to help retard and even reverse the frightening pace of the race to ruin.

Oh, for a revival, a renewal, a spiritual resurgence in the hearts of the church members until the churches will no longer be the most tragic unemployment centers in the land but centers of holy fire! Oh, that our churches may become centers of moral and spiritual renewal whose influence will fan out through our troubled cities and sweep across our revolt-torn campuses and into executive suites and labor temples and entertainment centers and political parties until sins are confessed and restitution is made! Only then can God begin to forgive our sins and to heal our land and to teach us once again that it is righteousness—not money, not bombs, not missiles—but that it is *righteousness* that exalteth a nation, or a church, or a person!

And what more appropriate time for all the unemployed saints in the churches to begin to pay the price of being "workers together with God" in such a redemptive task than on this Labor Day weekend?

Sorry, No Vacancy
(Christmas)

***And she brought forth her firstborn son, and wrapped him in swaddling clothes, and laid him in a manger; because there was no room for them in the inn* (Luke 2:7).**

Have you ever been travelling late at night and, upon finally deciding to turn in, found that most of the motels had turned on their "No Vacancy" signs?

As I prepare this message, I am in a famous inn just outside Tulsa, Okla. Their "No Vacancy" sign was on when I arrived, but I had reservations, so there was a room for me.

At this season of the year our minds turn to another inn—the inn at Bethlehem—an inn that had no room for the world's most distinguished couple, and so missed out on the honor of being the place of history's most important event—the birth of Christ.

Before you criticize the owner of that inn, however, please remember that he didn't know how important the couple were who wanted a room, and he had no computer reservations system by which to hold space for them. It was all on a "first come, first served" basis, and the inn was full, so Joseph and Mary had to move on—to a stable.

If you had been the owner of that inn, would you have made room for that couple that night? Or if you had been a guest at that inn, would you have given up your room so that this obviously poor couple could have a decent place in which their Child could be born?

That owner, and those guests, had legitimate excuse: they simply didn't know the historic significance of that couple, and that night, and that Baby.

To be sure, they were all expecting the Messiah to come sometime. But they certainly didn't expect Him to come that night, in that inn, in that way. As George MacDonald put it,

They all were looking for a king
To slay their foes and lift them high;
Thou cam'st, a little baby thing
That made a woman cry.

But we now *know* the significance of that couple and that night and that Babe. What is *our* excuse for hanging out the "No Vacancy" signs on the door of our hearts?

We know who that Baby was and why He came. We know that He was, and is, the Redeemer of the world. We know that He is Saviour, Lord, and coming King. We know of His words, His miracles, His love, His death on the Cross, His resurrection, His ascension, and His promise to return. We know all these things, and yet millions have no time for Him, no use for Him, no room for Him in their hearts or in their thoughts or in their lives. Their "No Vacancy" signs are on—and some do not care enough to even say, "Sorry."

Some, of course, are not that abrupt, that hard, that calloused, that final in their rejection. The majority have no ill will towards Christ. They think beautiful thoughts about Him; they even go to church occasionally and drop something into the collection plate, or in the Salvation Army kettles at Christmastime. But their minds and hearts and lives are saying, "Sorry; No Vacancy."

Their *minds* are so full of secular or sensual or scientific thoughts that there is simply no room for Christ—His insights, His ideals, His offers, and His demands.

Their *hearts* are so full of sin and selfishness and cynicism that there is no room for Christ—for His love, His forgiveness, His cleansing, His salvation.

Their *lives* are so full of things—things of school, of business; of promotion or position or prestige; of pleasures and people and possessions—that they simply have no room for Christ and the joy and fulfillment that only He can bring.

But, thank God, there are those whose minds and hearts and lives are not so crowded and cluttered and who have gladly made room for Christ. And not only have they made room, but have given Him *first* place—and *that,* of course, is the place He desires and deserves and demands.

That Christ who, on the night of His birth, found no room in the inn, and who during His life found no room in the hearts of His own people—*that* Christ still finds no room in the lives and homes of millions around the world. "He came unto his own," we are told, "but his own received him not. But," then and now, "as many as received him, to them gave he power to become the sons of God, even to them that believe on his name" (John 1:12).

That same Christ is just now standing at your heart's door—knocking, and saying, "Behold, I stand at the door, and knock: if any man hear my voice, and open the door, I will come in to him, and will sup with him, and he with me" (Rev. 3:20).

Unlike the innkeeper of long ago, you know who Jesus

is. You have heard Him knocking a long time. You have had your "No Vacancy" sign out long enough.

Let this Christmas season be the time when you finally take that sign down, won't you?

Open your heart's door to this matchless Guest and let Him come in. And even though He comes in as your *Guest*, He is really the rightful Owner, and before long the relationship changes and He becomes your *Host*. You become His Guest—in your own heart. Instead of trying to satisfy your deepest longings and hungers on the meager fare you can provide, you have the privilege of sitting at a table that Jesus spreads—and what He provides is nourishing to your mind, satisfying to your heart, and fulfilling to your life.

What a Guest! What a Host!

Let Him come in *now*, won't you?

4

In Search of the Authentic

A Relevant Gospel for An A-go-go Age

***For I am not ashamed of the gospel of Christ: for it is the power of God unto salvation to every one that believeth* (Rom. 1:16).**

The English," someone said, "gave the world the mini-skirt; the Germans gave the world the mini-bus; and the Israelis, the mini-war." Unfortunately, it could be added that some churches are giving the world mini-revivals, while others are preaching a mini-gospel.

But a mini-gospel is not adequate, or relevant, in a frantic and frivolous age.

And what is a "mini-gospel"?

It is an abbreviated one that requires no remorse, no repentance, no renunciation, no restitution—and promises no regeneration, no reconciliation, no rebirth, and no new life.

But that is not only an abbreviated gospel; it is an

emasculated one. It is a denial of the gospel Paul was talking about when he said, "I am not ashamed of the gospel of Christ: for it is the power of God unto salvation to every one that believeth" (Rom. 1:16).

To *everyone?* Yes. To the blacks and whites and browns and yellows; to those who live in ghettos as well as to those who live in suburbia; to the hippies in their communes, to the Hottentots in their huts, and to the high-ups in their penthouse apartments. The relevancy of the gospel does not depend on the century or the custom or the culture—whether primitive or "Playboy." The gospel is relevant anytime, anywhere, because it speaks to the basic hopes and hungers of humanity in every age and in every society.

It speaks not only of the disease, but of the remedy; not only of the problem, but of the solution; not only of the depths to which man has fallen, but of the heights to which he can attain. It talks not only about the successes and the certitudes, but about the risks and the failures; for it was Jesus who said that He had come, not "to call the righteous, but sinners to repentance."

In a success-oriented society that avidly follows all the fads and fancies of an a-go-go age, and seems to believe that every problem can be solved with a bullet or a bottle or a pill or a new hairdo or a bigger handout—in that kind of pepped-up society, the words sin, repentance, and salvation are not always popular.

But whether or not these are popular words, they are still relevant words in the vocabulary of redemption. For the only solution there has ever been for the problem of sin is the forgiving and healing love of God. And while that solution was not simple in its provision, it is simple in its appropriation.

"If I had known it was this simple," said the just-converted young wife as she stood by the altar, "I would have done this long ago." And her face and attitude revealed the astonished joy of finding God's forgiveness so satisfying and so simple.

Simple? Yes. But not cheap.

There has never been a shortcut to Calvary. There may be cut-rate *religion,* but there is no cut-rate *salvation* for anyone—anywhere—whether at an altar, or in a prayer tent, or in an inquiry room, or in any "soul winning made easy" gimmick of a religious salesman trying to rack up statistics in souls.

Jesus said, "Repent ye, and believe the gospel" (Mark 1:15). And that is still God's price tag for being saved, for being born again, for becoming a new creature in Christ. Repentance is saying, "I'm sorry for my sins, and I'm sorry enough to quit my sins, and I'm sorry enough to make restitution for past sins." Then, and only then, is one ready to "accept" Christ, for it is utterly impossible for any unrepentant soul to exercise *saving* faith.

The church—*any* church, in any age, a-go-go or otherwise—is remiss in its redemptive mission when it becomes nothing more than a religious discount house where right relationship with God is offered at a marked-down price. Too many are offering a "salvation" that requires nothing more than making a "decision" for Christ, or joining something, or memorizing a few verses of scripture, or giving mental assent to a few religious propositions, or exchanging one set of moral standards for another, or learning four, or five, or *50* religious "laws."

Anything less than repentance and faith is a marked-down price and all it buys is "cheap grace." For Jesus, who is "the same yesterday, and to day, and for ever," not only in His character, but in His demands, is still saying "Repent ye, and believe the gospel" (Mark 1:15); and, "Except ye repent, ye shall all likewise perish" (Luke 13:3).

And God, even in a soft and sassy age, has not turned soft on sin. But, oh, how tender He is with the sinner—if the sinner repents and believes! For in that moment God lifts him to a new level of life and reality, revealing new perspectives, giving new priorities, instilling new integrities. All of life becomes infused with new values, new certitudes, and atingle with new joys and new adventures and new fulfillments.

That become irrelevant?

Never! In *any* age.

You Can't Change Human Nature

***Therefore if any man be in Christ, he is a new creature: old things are passed away; behold; all things are become new* (II Cor. 5:17).**

Did you ever hear that statement, "You can't change human nature"? Of course you have, and many times.

How often that phrase is used to excuse all kinds of selfishness and stubbornness and greed and cruelty and lust and sin and even war itself!

"Oh, that's just human," people say with a shrug, "and you know you can't change human nature."

And so men continue to take advantage of others; continue to cheat, lie, and steal; continue to sacrifice every worthwhile value for the almighty dollar; and continue to plunder other men's businesses or homes or reputations or country. So the ghettos still swarm and stink, prejudice still erupts into hatred and violence, men are still denied their basic human dignities because of their color, millions still go to bed hungry every night, and minds are still darkened by ignorance. Quarrels continue to rage within families and neighborhoods and nations, and men who were created in God's image still kill other men who were also created in God's image.

And it's all explained away and excused and covered up by that hopeless shrug and the statement: "You can't change human nature."

Well, let's face it: *you* can't change human nature; neither can I; neither can any other man or woman on this planet.

You can educate a man; you can counsel with him; you can put nicer clothes on him, or place him in a bigger house or shinier car; you can promote him in his business or profession or labor or school or church; you can force-feed him culture and sophistication; but you can't change his *nature*.

He's still greedy and selfish and stubborn and lustful and cruel, and the thin veneer of culture and sophistication cannot hold that nature in check. For God said that the heart of man is wicked and deceitful above all things. The Apostle Paul said that "the carnal mind is enmity against God: for it is not subject to the law of God, neither indeed can be" (Rom. 8:7).

Just when you think you have the ape and the tiger educated out of him, or scared out of him, or shamed out of him, you will find that there is still considerable of the donkey left in him.

All attempts to change man's nature by outside pressures have failed. Even with his vast technical achievements and material advances and scientific discoveries, man still breaks out of those gossamer restraints and produces a Hiroshima or a Korea or a Vietnam, or a Watts, or a Detroit.

But while it is impossible for human nature to be

changed on merely the human level, that does not mean that it *can't* be changed.

God can change human nature!

He can, and He does.

How? He begins the change when He forgives the sins and the guilt that tyrannize and shackle and limit. For man was created to love God and to enjoy Him forever. Sin, which is rebellion against God, is foreign to his original nature, which was holy. For God created man holy and desired his fellowship in unbroken love and holiness. But in rebelling against God, man fell and his nature was corrupted.

But salvation is recovery, restoration, reconciliation. Then as man obeys and trusts God, surrendering every area of his life to God's will, God cleanses, purges, and purifies the inner nature until the heart is again at one with God. His body is still subject to disease; his mind is subject to mistake; his emotions are still subject to fatigue. But his nature is changed, rejuvenated, and aligned once again with God's love and will. He becomes, as Peter said, a partaker of His nature.

Don't you ever believe again that human nature can't be changed. *You* can't change it; *I* can't change it; no doctor or teacher or psychiatrist or chemist or philosopher can change it. But the eternal and loving and holy God *can* change it! And He *will,* if you will only let Him.

And how do you let Him?

Thank God, He's made it simple.

Confess your sins; tell Him you are sorry for your wrongdoing; forsake your sins, and believe His promise of forgiveness. Surrender your life, your loved ones, your job, your present, your future, your *self* completely to God and He will apply the cleansing merits of the blood of Christ to the sinful past. And in that moment He will give you a new heart, a new motive, a new point of view, a new heirarchy of values, a new set of priorities—and a new destiny. "For if any man be in Christ, Paul says, "he is a new creature: old things are passed away; behold, all things are become new" (II Cor. 5:17).

Think of it, Friend! Your nature can be so changed by the forgiving and cleansing blood of Christ until you are a partaker of *His* nature, and His nature is pure and holy. And as you follow Him and walk in the light, the blood of Jesus Christ, God's Son, will cleanse you from all sin (I John 1:7).

And this is happening all over the world, in any city or nation or continent where men submit to the lordship of Christ.

And it can happen to *you,* right now, wherever you are.

Seeing Is Believing

***And there were certain Greeks among them that came . . . to Philip . . . saying, Sir, we would see Jesus* (John 12:20-21).**

I don't know of anything that challenges me more than the words I sometimes see printed on plaques glued to pulpits or painted on the front of balconies—words taken from John's Gospel that say: "Sir, we would see Jesus."

Those words were originally spoken by some Greeks who were in Jerusalem. They had heard so much about Jesus that they finally asked Philip, one of the disciples, if he would take them to Jesus.

Ever since His birth, however, people have wanted to

see Jesus. The shepherds came to see Jesus while He was still in the manger. The wise men journeyed from the East to worship the Holy Child. And from that time till now, people of all classes, and from all cultures, have been saying, "We would see Jesus."

The Greeks who said those words to Philip were the product of a rich and noble heritage. All the philosophy and art and poetry and cultural resources of one of the highest civilizations the world has ever known were theirs. Yet they were conscious of a deep and fundamental need that all their wealth and wisdom and religion had never filled. Their minds were full of knowledge and their pockets were full of money, but their hearts were still void of the reality and meaning which alone make life worthwhile. With all their sophistication, they still had a God-shaped blank at the center of their lives.

But isn't that our condition today? We too have more things and fewer values, more money and less meaning, more power and less purpose than any generation in history. In spite of all our science and the gadgets and knowledge and trappings of a proud and affluent society, we still have a God-shaped blank at the center of our lives.

Other generations may have been God-intoxicated; ours is God-starved. And increasing numbers of men and women everywhere are saying, "Sir, we would see Jesus."

May God have mercy on the churches and the preachers who try to answer this cry with pet political philosophies, or with fancy social schemes, or with theological mumbo-jumbo that dethrones God and denies the deity of His Son—a pseudo religion that distorts the meaning of His shed blood, dilutes His demands, and smothers the real Christ in religious red tape and holy-sounding double-talk.

No wonder so many people are dropping out of the institutional church today. They looked up so often and were not fed. They cried so repeatedly, "Sir, we would see Jesus";

but instead of being confronted with Christ they were told how to vote, or which politician to campaign for, or which sign to carry, or how little they needed to believe and still be accepted in the church. Or they heard the perpetual promotion of a multitude of picayune and petty programs that minister more to human pride and denominational prestige than to God's glory.

The Church is in the world, not to compete with other institutions on the basis of size or finance or prestige, but to proclaim Christ and to advance His cause in the world.

And when hungry-hearted men and women and confused young people come to church and look up, they don't expect to see or hear some clerical Walter Cronkite merely reporting the secular news or commenting on it. They are saying, "*Sir, we would see Jesus.* We hear enough about riots and violence and atrocities and all the sordid accounts of political and labor and business shenanigans during the week. We want to hear a word from God."

They are saying, "We have heard enough questions; we want to hear some answers. We have heard enough diagnoses; we want to hear about some cures. We are fed up to here with human replies and opinions; we want something with the stamp of the eternal upon it—*Sir, we would see Jesus!*"

In John Wesley's *Journal,* there is this recurring phrase which summed up his daily activities: "I gave them Christ."

What a sweeping revival of religion might occur today, with its resultant improvement in morals—in government and business and labor and schools and homes and in personal living—if all preachers were able to sum up their daily activities with, "I gave them Christ"!

This same Philip who, with Andrew, took the Greeks to Jesus, also said to skeptical but hungry-hearted Nathanael: "Come and see [Jesus]." Philip knew that Jesus was His own best argument; that Jesus was His own best credential;

that Jesus was self-authenticating. One look at Jesus, he knew, would do more than all the theories about Him could ever do.

And so I say to you today, wherever you are, and whatever your need: "Come and see. Come and see Jesus. Come and see how wonderful He really is. Come and see if He isn't all you ever hoped God would be. Come and see if He won't lift your heavy load of guilt and give you the reality and meaning and purpose and fulfillment you have always longed for."

Oh, if I were only able to lift Jesus up as I feel He should be lifted up, and to proclaim Him as He should be proclaimed, I believe every needy and hungry heart would do as Thomas did: fall at His feet and exclaim in surrender and faith, "My Lord and my God."

Yes, to see Him—to really *see* Him—is to believe Him.

And if seeing Him with the eye of faith means so much to us today, think what it will be like when we see Him face-to-face!

No wonder that John could say, in awe and wonder and faith: "Beloved, now are we the sons of God, and it doth not yet appear what we shall be: but we know that, when he shall appear, we shall be like him; for we shall see him as he is" (I John 3:2).

Under New Management

***If any man be in Christ, he is a new creature: old things are passed away; behold, all things are become new* (II Cor. 5:17).**

Surely you have seen those notices in front of restaurants and gas stations and motels announcing that the business is "under new management."

That announcement is usually made to assure the public that, although service had deteriorated and the entire operation had become careless and inefficient, now, under new management, things are improved—even though sometimes the "improvement" involves only a new coat of paint or a rearrangement of the clutter around the cash register.

But a *life* that has deteriorated needs more than a surface change. It needs to be brought under new control, new direction, new management. And this is the miracle that happens when one becomes a "new creature in Christ."

This spiritual change is not cosmetic; it is surgical. It goes so deep and transforms so radically that one can begin to sing,

What a wonderful change in my life has been wrought,
Since Jesus came into my heart!

I have heard thousands sing that song, and I have heard many tell how and when the change came about. And always —*always*—the change came, the transformation occurred, when they said "yes" to Christ and came under His control and began living under His "management."

There is that young marine, for instance, who had returned from Vietnam. He found that his frustrations and sense of futility had not all been caused by the mud and heat and wretched conditions of his environment overseas. For even after he was home, he still had not found himself. He felt, as he said, "like a wheel that was all spokes and no hub."

But God used a sermon to show that young man that God has a purpose for every life and that no life can be happy and fulfilled outside of God's purpose. That truth got through to him and he came forward and accepted Christ. In that moment he became a "new creature," with his past forgiven, and a new life opening up before him.

That was eight months ago, and now, under new management, he is in college preparing for a life of service. He has a sense of commitment and direction that surprises even himself.

Another who recently came "under new management" is a woman in her late thirties, twice-divorced, and on the verge of becoming an alcoholic. Her life was going to pieces and she seemingly could do nothing about it.

What was the solution? More alcohol? Narcotics? A new husband? A changed environment?

No. The real solution is never any of these. Her only hope was placing herself under new management—allowing Christ to come into her heart and free her from the tyranny of the past, to bring organization out of inner chaos, and to give her a real reason for living.

To "manage," as Webster defines it, is to "control and direct." And there are multitudes who, under their own control and direction, find their lives deteriorating and on the brink of collapse. Frantically but futilely they are trying to blot out their guilt and fear and insecurity and mental or marital hang-ups in liquor or sex or dope.

But the good news of the gospel is that no one needs to continue in that direction. There is an option!

And Christ is that option. He is the alternative to futility, to the tyranny of sin, to the threats and fears that paralyze life and plague and plunder the emotions.

Whenever *anyone* throws down the weapons of resistance and admits his failure and his defeat and allows Christ to take control of his life, he becomes a new person, under new management. He begins to live on a new level, with new directions and new goals. He is engaged in an exciting adventure that he never knew existed before, through a grace he never experienced before.

To become a new creature, under new management, is not merely to be improved or reformed or altered externally. It is to be remade. It is to be different even from what one was at his best. It is more than forgiveness of the past; it is more than the removal of guilt; it is reconciliation—which means the restoration of a relationship.

When we are born again and come under this new management of Christ, we can say, with the Apostle Paul, "Old things are passed away; behold, all things are become new" (II Cor. 5:17). We find that the "old" desires and purposes of a self-centered life have given way to the "new" desires and purposes of a Christ-centered life.

Our outlook is changed, our frame of reference is altered, our values and priorities are transformed. We find that money and pleasure and position and prestige cease to have the old attraction for us, while love and duty and the devotional life are becoming more and more important and alluring.

And to continue to live under Christ's management will mean that we not only have the continuing assurance of sins forgiven, but that we will enjoy the continuing and increasing assurance of His leadership, His guidance, His love, and His grace. That grace, as the Apostle Paul found, will always be sufficient, as long as we live in God's will and under His management.

Accept Him then, won't you? You'll find that He's not only a great Saviour, but that He's also a great Manager.

Some Things Haven't Changed

***For all have sinned, and come short of the glory of God* (Rom. 3:23).**
***God commendeth his love toward us, in that, while we were yet sinners, Christ died for us* (Rom. 5:8).**

Perhaps you have heard of the professor in a large medical school in the East who closes his last lecture to each of his classes with these words: "I have given you the best information available. The textbooks we have used are the most reliable and widely accepted. But before we part company, I must caution you that the science of medicine is developing so rapidly that, in a few years from now, perhaps half the things I have taught you won't be so. Unfortunately, I don't know which half that will be."

Change is one of the fundamental facts of life, in any age. In the nineteenth century, for instance, Goethe, the German philosopher, said, "It is most disagreeable that one cannot nowadays learn a thing once and for all, and have done with it." What would he say about the incredible changes in this latter half of the twentieth century?

While many things on the surface of life and on the margins of knowledge may change from age to age, or from year to year, yet there are at least two things that haven't changed: man's problem, and God's answer.

And what is man's basic problem? Vietnam? Inflation? Communism? Poverty? Bigotry? Ignorance? No. All of these are complex and urgent problems, certainly, but they are spin-offs from man's basic problem, which is still sin.

It is of course unfashionable to even pronounce the word "sin" these days. It is much more polite to talk of maladjustment, or glandular imbalance, or mental or emotional illness. "Don't even say 'sin,' is the plea. Call it stupidity or sickness or delinquency or disease—just don't call it "sin."

Let a man run off with another woman, but don't call him wicked; call him weak. Let a young, unmarried girl get pregnant, but don't say she sinned; just say she made a mistake. Let some young hoodlums wreck a house or a school or a church or a life, but don't say they are bad; just say they are bored. Let a whole group defy all authority and flaunt their debaucheries by going around filthy and ragged as they literally go to "pot," but don't call them depraved; just say they are deprived. Let men and women riot and rampage and burn and loot and throw bricks and bottles filled with filth at the policemen who try to stop them—but don't call them thieves and murderers; just call it police brutality, or society's failure. Let men who have risen to the highest levels of labor or business or government get caught with their hands in the till, but don't call them criminals; just call them clever. Let nations rise against nations and gut cities with their bombs and murder and maim civilians and soldiers with their bullets, but don't call it war; just call it keeping the peace.

When, oh, when, will somebody, somewhere, have the courage to stand up and say that *sin* is at the bottom of it all! Where in all this sinful and shattered world is the man who will slash through all the fancy talk and slick sham and say that lying and thievery and killing and hatred and perversion and adultery are all *sins*. Not mistakes, not weaknesses, not maladjustment, not disease, not ignorance—but sins! Sins against God and sins against humanity.

Changing the vocabulary doesn't change the problem. Man's basic problem is still sin—a sinful nature, a sinful heart, an inherent rebelliousness against God and righteousness.

And no amount of education has been able to change that. No amount of affluence has been able to change it. No amount of cleverness has been able to change it. No number of bombs or missiles or spacecraft or computers have been able to change it. For man is still sinful, and it is still true, as Jeremiah said, that "the heart is deceitful above all things, and desperately wicked: who can know it?" (Jer. 17:9)

Who, indeed, but God! And, oh, how He knows it!

For man's sin rises as a stench in the nostrils of God, and He hates it—a holy God would have to hate sin. No matter how high man, with his intellect, may climb the stairs toward his own utopia, God still sees the filth and slime of sin in the basement of the human heart. And no amount of philanthropy or psychology or religion or do-goodism can hide that sin from God, or lessen His hatred of it.

But while God hates sin, He still loves the sinner. And that is still God's answer to man's deepest problem: love—love expressed not in a theory or a philosophy or a theology, but love expressed in a Person—the Person, Jesus Christ.

"For God so loved the world, that he gave his only begotten Son, that whosoever believeth in him should not perish, but have everlasting life" (John 3:16). "But God commendeth his love toward us, in that, while we were yet sinners, Christ died for us" (Rom. 5:8). "For the wages of sin is death; but the gift of God is eternal life through Jesus Christ our Lord" (Rom. 6:23).

In all the swift changes of a changing world, God's love hasn't changed. And His unchanging love is the only answer to the world's need that there is.

To the question, "What can wash away my sins?" humanity has heard only one answer: "Nothing but the blood of Jesus." To that age-old companion question, "What can make me whole again?" there has ever been but one answer: "Nothing but the blood of Jesus."

No wonder, then, that through the years as men and women have knelt at the foot of the cross of Christ and experienced, through forgiveness and cleansing, God's answer to their deepest problem, they have been able to rise and go on their way singing,

Oh precious is the flow
That makes me white as snow!
No other fount I know,
Nothing but the blood of Jesus.

And that, dear friends, is still God's answer, and the *only* answer, to man's deepest problem.

5

This Way to Maturity

End of Improvement

So shall we all at last attain to the unity inherent in our faith and our knowledge of the Son of God—to mature manhood, measured by nothing less than the full stature of Christ **(Eph. 4:13, NEB).**

A few days ago, as I was driving from Little Rock, Ark., to Kansas City, I noticed that in a number of places crews were at work on the road. There were the usual signs saying, "Construction Ahead," or, "Road Repairs; Drive Slowly."

At the end of each stretch of road being repaired or rebuilt, there would be a sign saying, "END OF IMPROVEMENT. Thank You."

But not only are those words found on signs along the

highways; they are written across the attitudes and faces of far too many people—people who have stopped growing, stopped improving, and are no longer challenged by new adventures or excited by new opportunities for growth and fulfillment.

It is Karen Horney, the psychiatrist, who reminds us that "the task of life is to grow, and to keep on growing as long as life lasts." And that "old age sets in only when there is no longer any growth of mind or personality."

But it is not only old age that sets in; it is stagnation and death that set in when one erects the sign: "End of Improvement." For when anyone ceases to grow, to improve, to advance, to develop, he begins to die.

"A mature person," says Overstreet, "is not one who has come to a certain level of achievement and stopped there. He is rather a *maturing person*—one whose *linkages with life* are constantly becoming stronger and richer because his attitudes are such as to encourage their growth rather than their stoppage." What is the chief end of man? Overstreet answers, "To move toward wholeness of life."

That answer in no way contradicts the Christian concept that the chief end of man is to "glorify God and enjoy Him forever." For it is only the man who is developing, improving, and moving in the direction of wholeness and ever larger fulfillments of life that can really glorify God.

"The path of the just," God says, "is as the shining light, that shineth more and more unto the perfect day" (Prov. 4:18). And it is only as one walks in that increasing light that one can enjoy right relationship with God and can grow as he should. Only thus can come the improvement and development of that more abundant life of which Jesus is both Pattern and Provision.

"End of Improvement" signs can be seen everywhere today. You can see them on college campuses, especially at commencement time; you can see them in executive suites, where men have run out of challenge; you can see them in factories, where men no longer try to improve their skills; you can see them in hospitals, where men no longer hope; you can see them in homes, where love has not been nurtured and the marriage has gone stale and sour.

But, of course, the place where these "End of Improvement" signs are most disappointing and damaging is in the churches.

Multitudes of professing Christians have erected the sign, "End of Improvement," and have literally stopped growing, stopped advancing, stopped improving. They have become impervious even to the challenge to make their faith up-to-date and relevant.

The urgent and pressing economic, social, and racial needs of life today make no impression on Christians who have stopped growing. They retreat into their churches and sing hymns and nod at sermons and pat each other on the back—while their world deteriorates and their cities burn and their schools are disrupted and the whole fabric of their society is torn to shreds.

Some Christians have posted "End of Improvement" signs alongside their personal religious experiences. They have made an initial commitment to Christ or the church, but they have stopped there. They have ceased to grow, to develop, to be open to new insights, or to be challenged by deeper penetrations of the Spirit.

Others have placed "End of Improvement" signs by a second religious experience, and because they profess to be sanctified, they apparently feel that they have reached the destination and that all spiritual progress is at an end.

Oswald Chambers has a word for people like that when he says, "People stagnate because they never get beyond the image of their experiences into the life of God which transcends all experiences."

And commenting on Bushnall's phrase, "magnitudes

beyond the narrows," Dr. J. B. Chapman said, "The gate of repentance is a narrow gate, but beyond the gate are expansive plains of pardon and peace. The gate of full consecration likewise is narrow, but beyond the gate is Beulah Land."

Michelangelo's lifelong motto was, "*Ancora imparo*"—"Still I am learning." And this must be the motto of every Christian. After conversion, and after sanctification, and after years of living for Christ, the Christian will continue to say, "I am still learning more about Christ, more about His love, more about His will for me."

And even in heaven there will be no place for "End of Improvement" signs. The challenge and adventure of eternity will not be merely eating fruit and living in mansions, but rather the possibility of continued improvement, continued development toward "the measure of the stature of the fulness of Christ."

How High Does Your Ladder Reach?

***Forgetting those things which are behind, and reaching forth unto those things which are before, I press toward the mark for the prize of the high calling of God in Christ Jesus* (Phil. 3:13-14).**

I've got my future all planned," said a young man to his college professor. "When I get out of school, I intend to make a lot of money."

"And what then?" asked the professor.

"Well, I will then get married and perhaps travel around the world."

The professor nodded and asked, "And then?"

"Well, then I'll probably settle down and just enjoy life."

"And then?" said the professor.

"Well, I suppose, like everyone else, I'll grow old and then, of course, die."

The professor looked straight into the student's eyes and asked, "And then?"

The young man frowned, and was silent. He had no answer to that last "And then?"

In other words, his ladder did not reach to heaven.

And no matter who you are, or how high your ladder reaches, if it doesn't reach to heaven, it doesn't reach high enough.

There are many attractive rungs where one can stop, and the lure of the immediate goal is often overwhelming. But to stop there is damaging, and ultimately damning.

Many thousands of young people, entering school, will have ladders reaching only as high as a diploma or a degree. But no matter how high the degree, to stop climbing just because one reaches that rung is ruinous because it thwarts the inner urge for continued growth. Not all Ph.D.'s are happy or fulfilled.

Others have ladders that reach only as high as the bank. But after one has made a lot of money, where does he go from there? One young man, making big money, quit his position with a large corporation and started teaching school. And why? Because he said that he had come to the conclusion that life should represent something more important than the mere ability to make money.

Others have ladders that reach only as high as the headlines. But that is never high enough. Dr. Moran, Winston

Churchill's personal physician, said in his diary that even when Churchill was in his eighties, if in scanning the morning paper he failed to see his name anywhere, he was peeved and his day was ruined. Fame, no matter how great or how continuous, is never enough to make life meaningful and worthwhile.

Others have ladders that reach only as high as the chairman's or president's chair. The lust for power is a strange and corrosive drive. And yet there are those who are willing to sacrifice every worthwhile value to rise one more rung on the corporate or political or ecclesiastical ladder. That rung of power seems so attractive that they will ruthlessly step on the fingers, or neck, or heart of anyone who gets in their way.

But the peak is an exposed spot, and is open to attack from all sides. Also the descent can be much swifter than the ascent. And many have forgotten, to their sorrow, the old advice: You'd better be nice to everyone on your way up, because you're going to meet the same people on your way down.

Many others, of course, have ladders that reach as high as a creed, or an ethic, or a church. But part of the disillusionment of our times is due to the discovery that a ladder that reaches only as high as a doctrine or a discipline or a denomination doesn't reach nearly high enough.

And so, instead of climbing on up in genuine repentance and faith to the reality of personal experience in Christ, they have jumped off their ladder and announced that there was nothing "up there."

How absurd for anyone, be he theologian, or preacher, or layman, to say that there is nothing "up there" when he has not taken the trouble, or been willing to pay the price in humility and obedience, to climb up and find out.

If the rungs of creeds or rules or experiences do not lead one up to Christ and a personal experience of His love and

His forgiveness and His cleansing, then the very rungs have been a hindrance, for they have been the occasion of his arrested development.

To you, then, who are saying, "I think I will start attending some church," I say, "Fine. But what then?" To you who are saying, "I'm going to start living a better life," I say, "Splendid. But what then?" To you who have been giving mere intellectual assent to certain beliefs, even orthodox beliefs, and are trusting your eternal salvation to such mental affirmation, I say, "Well and good. But that isn't enough—that ladder doesn't even begin to reach high enough."

No one's ladder—no matter how beautiful or expensive or wonderfully built—will ever reach high enough unless it begins at Calvary and has rungs that reach to heaven.

For God said that "all have sinned, and come short of the glory of God" (Rom. 3:23). And unless you repent of your sins and accept Christ as Lord and Saviour, you will never reach even the first decisive rung on the ladder.

On a memorial tablet high up in the Swiss Alps there is the name of a famous climber who went out one day never to return. Underneath the man's name are these simple words: "He died climbing."

That should be, and had better be, the epitaph to every life that wants to make it from earth to heaven.

Just how high does *your* ladder reach? If it doesn't begin at Calvary and reach to heaven, you'd better get another ladder—or through repentance and surrender and faith allow God to add the necessary rungs to the one you have.

The Pollution Problem

Wherefore Jesus also, that he might sanctify the people with his own blood, suffered without the gate **(Heb. 13:12).**

One can hardly pick up a newspaper or a magazine these days without seeing an article warning of the increasing danger of water and air pollution. The pollution problem seems to be one of the more disturbing side effects of the population explosion.

That irritating combination of smoke and car-exhaust called "smog" has been the subject of comedians' jokes for a long while. But it is no longer funny when 400 people die of it in one two-week period in New York City. It is not amusing when eyes burn, and nostrils itch, and throats tingle as people find it increasingly difficult to breathe in such polluted atmosphere. And it is no longer a joke when magazines like *Life* devote entire pages to show pictures of dead fish and dying wildlife littering the banks of polluted streams and beaches.

But this so-called "pollution problem" has been around for a long time. In fact, it's been with us from the very beginning of the human race. It didn't start in Los Angeles or Pittsburgh or New York. It started in the Garden of Eden.

For when our first parents sinned against God, at that moment human nature became polluted. And that pollution has been passed through all the generations of man through all the centuries. Every human being has come into the world with a polluted, contaminated, fallen, sinful nature.

And it is *that* pollution problem that is the most disastrous, disturbing, and ultimately damning problem that faces mankind.

The Apostle Paul gives the dimensions of this pollution when he speaks of men "being filled with all unrighteousness, fornication, wickedness, covetousness, maliciousness; full of envy, murder, debate, deceit, malignity; whisperers, backbiters, haters of God, despiteful, proud, boasters, inventors of evil things, disobedient to parents, without understanding, covenantbreakers, without natural affection, implacable, unmerciful" (Rom. 1:29-31).

Talk about pollution—what is smog, or scummy water, compared with that?

While commissions have recently been formed and committees appointed and millions of dollars allocated in Washington, and elsewhere, to seek a solution to the problem of polluted air and water, men have been trying to cope with the pollution of their hearts for a long, long time.

They have tried, for instance, to educate pollution out of their nature. Over a hundred years ago Horace Mann prophesied in Boston that crime would be wiped out with the increase in size and number of tax-supported schools. Well, we have the biggest tax-supported school system in history —but we also have the highest crime rate in history, with jails crowded and prisons jammed and violence of every kind stalking the streets.

"The greatest disappointment in America," said Dr. Charles E. Jefferson, "is the fact that we have poured billions of dollars into public education and have turned out a generation of pagans."

To a nation and a world disturbed and anxious about the pollution problem, I have good news! There is a solution. God has already solved the problem—and His solution is the forgiving, cleansing merits of the blood of Jesus Christ!

It was Zechariah who prophesied that "in that day there shall be a fountain opened to the house of David . . . for sin and for uncleanness" (Zech. 13:1).

The Apostle Paul verifies that this fountain has been opened and reasons that "if the blood of bulls and of goats sanctifieth to the purifying of the flesh: how much more shall the blood of Christ purge your conscience from dead works to serve the living God?" (Heb. 9:13-14)

Years after Pentecost, Peter was still testifying that hearts were purified, cleansed, purged, and filled with a new power on the Day of Pentecost. And thousands of men and women since that time have witnessed that, in response to their consecration and faith, God's Holy Spirit applied the cleansing merits of the blood of Christ to the very core of their beings. In that moment there came to them a consciousness, an awareness, a reality of cleanness, of purity, and of wholeness that they had never experienced before.

The pollution problem of the human heart cannot be solved by a committee from Washington. Billions of dollars can't solve it. Better housing can't solve it. Fatter paychecks can't solve it. Moving to the right side of the tracks can't solve it. Joining a church can't solve it.

The only real solution to the problem of the pollution of the human heart is the one provided by God in the atoning, cleansing, purifying power of the blood of Christ.

Praise God! There is a solution! But you could stand by Niagara and die of thirst—if you didn't drink the water. You could sit by loaded tables at a smorgasbord and die of hunger—if you refused to eat. You could sit on the steps of Mayo's in Rochester and die of disease—if you didn't avail yourself of their treatment.

Accept God's solution for sin and uncleanness today, then, won't you? Confess your sins, and believe Him to forgive your sins. Then surrender your all to Him, and find your very nature purged of the pollution of inbred sin. And as you walk in the light, His blood will continue to cleanse you from all sin (I John 1:7). You will find that you, too, can sing:

Down at the cross where my Savior died,
Down where for cleansing from sin I cried;
There to my heart was the blood applied,
Glory to His name!

Learn to Live Beyond Your Means

***Ye shall receive power, after that the Holy Ghost is come upon you, and ye shall be witnesses unto me . . . unto the uttermost part of the earth* (Acts 1:8).**

With a national debt of over $350 billion, it is apparent that for a long time now the United States has been living beyond its means.

In fact, "our real problems," says Robert Maynard Hutchins, "are concealed from us by our current remarkable prosperity . . . which is based on our buying things from each other that we do not want, at prices we cannot pay, on terms we cannot meet, because of advertising we do not believe."

Living beyond our means may be bad economics, but it is good religion. In fact, those through history who have amounted to anything for God and His cause have been those who lived beyond their means, beyond their resources, beyond their abilities, beyond their strengths. The point is that they dared to risk everything for God and found that, when they came to the end of their human resources, there was a limitless supply available from God's storehouse.

That same power of God is available today to everyone

who is faced with problems too complex for his understanding, with tasks too big for his resources, and with situations too difficult for his cleverness.

Is it any wonder that so much of our effort for God is impotent and fruitless when we so seldom attempt anything that requires any more strength than we ourselves possess? It is when we are willing to commit ourselves to a quality of life beyond our means, and to a task greater than our resources would justify, that we are privileged to draw upon God's unlimited supply of power.

The world simply cannot be challenged, or even be interested, in the kind of Christian life demonstrated by the timid, tepid, careful, and calculating followers of Christ who can do what they do without any help at all from God. It requires no divine help to attend church, support good causes, teach a class, serve on a committee, sing in the choir, or be nice and decent.

It does require resources beyond the human, however, to meet life with a margin, to be vibrant and victorious in life's battles, and to be a relevant and effective witness to the reality of Christ in the heart.

And this power beyond the human is exactly what Jesus promised when He said, "Ye shall receive power, after that the Holy Ghost is come upon you: and ye shall be witnesses unto me." That means everywhere you go. Why skimp along on your meager resources, then, when Christ gives you the privilege of writing checks on heaven's bank?

Please notice, however, that Jesus did not say that we were to be witnesses merely to a doctrine, or to a rule, or to an institution. One can be a witness to all those without any help at all from God.

He did say that we were to be witnesses unto Him. And if Christ is to be glorified in our lives, if we are to be effective witnesses to the grace of God in our hearts, we will have to live beyond our means through the power of the Holy Spirit.

He alone can enable us to be victorious in life's emergencies and make us effective in our service. "In all these things," Paul said, "we are more than conquerors through him that loved us" (Rom. 8:37). And whatever we really accomplish for God, Paul insists, we will accomplish by the power of God which works within us. (Phil. 2:13).

It is lamentable that so many limit the realities of this power to a once-and-for-all experience, when God wants to pour out this power, this unction, this enduement, again and again.

The disciples were filled on the Day of Pentecost. But in Acts 4:8 and again in Acts 4:31, we read that the disciples were again filled with the Holy Ghost. Both Paul and Barnabas were filled with the Holy Spirit at widely different periods of their lives.

Purity of course is a constant, but power is a variable. Peter testified to the end of his life that his heart was purified on the Day of Pentecost; but Peter received fresh enduements of power, fresh unctions, fresh outpourings of the Holy Spirit after Pentecost.

It is Dr. Adam Clarke who reminds us that, though "these disciples had received the Holy Spirit on the day of Pentecost, yet they were capable of larger communications; and what they had then received did not preclude the necessity of frequent supplies on emergent occasions. Indeed," he says, "one communication of this Spirit always makes way and disposes for another. For neither apostle nor private Christian can subsist in the Divine life without frequent influences from on high."

Dr. J. B. Chapman emphasized the possibility, indeed the necessity, of frequent enduements of power when he said, "There is no single act of faith that answers for all time. If we could get spiritual supplies for an extended period, perhaps we . . . would forget to come to our Heavenly

Father for that companionship which is of greater consequence than any detached 'blessing' which could possibly come to us."

One baptism, yes, but many fresh outpourings. One baptism, but many fresh unctions.

Learn to live, then, beyond your means. Attempt things for God that require more than your resources can justify. Live by great commitments and loving responses that require strengths and power beyond your own—power that comes only from God.

Live within your means economically and physically and emotionally, but *spiritually* learn to live beyond your means, knowing that there has never been a drain on heaven's resources and that God's bank has never gone bankrupt—and never will.

Going a Little Farther

And he went a little farther, and fell on his face, and prayed, saying, O my Father, if it be possible, let this cup pass from me: nevertheless not as I will, but as thou wilt **(Matt. 26:39).**

A famous swimming coach who has produced a number of national champions was asked the secret of his amazing record. "There is no particular secret," he said. "We just operate on three words: hurt, pain, and agony."

He went on to explain that those athletes who worked out until they hurt a little always improved some, and that those who worked on until they were in pain would reach a higher level of superiority. But that those who were strongly enough motivated and had the drive to keep on working out until they could barely lift an arm and were in sheer agony —"*There,*" the coach concluded, "is where champions are made."

And it is that willingness to go a little farther, to practice a little more, to work a little longer, that always distinguishes those who excel from those who merely do well.

It never costs much, you see, to move from poor to average. It isn't even very costly to move from average to good. Where the real price must be paid—and where the greatest fulfillment comes—is in moving from good to best. And that always means "going a little farther."

The real achievement in any field, however, is not merely to be superior to others—that could be an accident of birth. The real achievement is in constantly exceeding one's previous best. And that, also, requires "going a little farther."

It is not surprising to read in Matthew's Gospel that Jesus "went a little farther, and fell on his face, and prayed, saying, O my Father, if it be possible, let this cup pass from me: nevertheless not as I will, but as thou wilt" (Matt. 26:39).

Jesus stood with his disciples at the entrance to the Garden of Gethsemane. After impressing them with the urgency of that hour, He asked Peter and James and John to come apart with Him to pray. But then Jesus left even those three and went on "a little farther." That is always the price of leadership—the willingness, the concern, the courage, the stamina, to go on "a little farther" than others can, or will, go.

As Longfellow said,

The heights by great men reached and kept
Were not attained by sudden flight,

But they, while their companions slept,
Were toiling upward in the night.

In other words, there is no automatic success. The price of making a worthwhile contribution in life is always to go beyond what is easy, to go beyond what is expected or necessary—to go "a little farther."

This, of course, is not a pleasant or popular truth in this easygoing day of ours. This is a time when discipline is discounted. Increasing numbers are more interested in security than in opportunity, in comfort than in effort, in the easy satisfactions of mediocrity than in the rich fulfillments of achievement. Popular phrases of the day are: "Take it easy"; and, "Can you get it for me wholesale?"

In fact, life at times seems to resemble nothing so much as a vast discount house, where a person feels either stupid or cheated if he has to pay the full price for anything.

And yet, meaningful life, fulfilled life, creative or redemptive life, can never be bought at discount prices. That quality of life is always in stock, but it is never on sale.

The dedication and the discipline and the drive of the achievers in any field—whether in art or sports or scholarship or politics or science—should be a challenge to, and a judgment upon, all those professing Christians who become satisfied with merely being moral or decent or respectable or religious. The heights of real goodness, of real spirituality, of real effectiveness, could be attained if they were willing to go "a little farther" in their devotion, in their commitment, and in all the disciplines of Christian living.

In the book about her mother, the daughter of Madame Curie recounts the endless experiments tried by her parents, Pierre and Madame Curie. She tells that after the four hundred eighty-seventh experiment had failed, Pierre gave up in despair, crying, "It can't be done; it can't be done! Maybe in a hundred years it can be done but never in our lifetime."

But Madame Curie, with quiet determination, answered,

"If it takes a hundred years it will be a pity, but I dare not do less than work for it so long as I have life."

With so many complex problems in the world still unsolved, with so many important tasks yet unfinished and so many needs still unmet and so many souls yet unsaved, shall we, dare we, as Christians, be less dedicated or determined than *that* in the light of our own potential and the urgencies of our times?

As followers of that Christ who was always willing to go "a little farther," may we be willing in this our day to pray a little harder, give a little more, dig a little deeper, love a little more—to see divisions healed, broken lives mended, sin-sick souls saved, and a world that is filled with evil and hatred and violence brought under the mastery and lordship of Jesus Christ.

Unusual times demand unusual living, and when the world is at its worst, Christians should be willing to pay whatever price is necessary to be at their best.

6

For God and Country

The Church—Who Needs It?

Let us speak the truth in love; so shall we fully grow up into Christ. He is the head, and on him the whole body depends **(Eph. 4:15, NEB).**

Everyone is familiar by now with Walter Shirra's commercial for the American railroads in which he asks, "The railroads—who needs them?" and then answers, "You do. We all do."

Astronaut Wally Shirra may be the only one asking that question about the *railroads*, but increasing thousands are asking that question today about the *Church*.

Seldom in its long history has the Christian Church been under more fire, been questioned more critically, suffered more prominent defections, or had its very existence threatened or challenged by more diverse segments of society than at the present time.

The appearance and growth of religious groups outside the framework of the institutional Church are given wide publicity, while Gallup Polls and Harris Surveys reveal not only the decline in church attendance, but the erosion of faith in, and commitment to, the Church itself. A recent religious survey by the *Ladies Home Journal*, for instance, was reported under the title, "You Can't Find God in Church Anymore."

With the increasing criticism of the institutional Church and the spreading apathy towards all forms of organized religion, the question might well be asked: "The Church—who needs it?"

Well, no one needs it—if the Church is just another secular institution competing with other institutions on the basis of size or finances or prestige or secular power or social action.

No one needs the Church—if it is merely a religious club reflecting the mores and morals and manners of the world around it. Martin Marty, among others, warns of the danger and the tragedy of the Church, chameleon-like, taking on the coloration of its secular environment and thus having its prophetic note so muted and muffled that it can no longer bring the world under judgment.

No one needs the church—if it doesn't proclaim the gospel. And how can it proclaim the gospel which is "the power of God unto salvation" if it no longer believes in the deity of Jesus Christ, or if it ridicules the redemptive power of His blood, or if it denies or distorts the personality and ministry of the Holy Spirit?

No one needs the church—if it is to be nothing more than another entertainment hall where second-rate entertainers who couldn't make it in Hollywood are now salvaging their egos by working the religious side of the street. Within the sacred precincts of the sanctuary "rock" bands now beat and electric guitars wail and singers gyrate in all the sensuous writhings of fertility rites more appropriate in the Congo than in the house of God.

No! If that is all the Church is, then *no one* needs it.

But that is *not* the *Church!* That is a travesty of the Church. For that kind of organization is not only a distortion; it is a denial of everything the Church of Jesus Christ stands for and is in the world to do.

The Church was meant to be a *redemptive agency* a place where men would be confronted with God's Word both in judgment and in love. It is a place where Christ is lifted up as Saviour and Lord. It is a fellowship in which those who accept Christ can develop that relationship and, in turn, under the anointing of God's Spirit, go out to influence others to accept Christ.

It is redeemed men who will redeem society. No amount of money or handouts or guns or bombs or missiles or welfare programs or education will do it. It is when men are transformed by the living Christ that they will transform their society. Science can make our world a *neighborhood,* but only a church producing redeemed men can make it a *brotherhood.*

Dean Willard Sperry of Harvard said, "The world seeks the Church . . . at those times when life matters most." And it is in the deep hours, the troubled hours, the challenging hours, that men most realize their need of true values, of real priorities, of great commitments, and of the eternal dimensions of life. And it is the Church, when it is true to its Lord, that continually confronts and challenges men with those realities.

The Church—who needs it? You do. We all do. For the Church is the only institution in our civilization whose *primary* purpose is to keep alive the moral and spiritual principles without which a decent world is impossible.

Who needs the Church? You do. We all do. The Bible tells us that even Jesus "went to the synagogue, as his custom was, on the sabbath day." And that same Bible says, Forsake not "the assembling of yourselves together." It is in church where we most often find our worst selves confronted by our better selves, and our better selves confronted by Christ who is better yet. And there, yielding to that Christ, we experience a transformation of character that profoundly affects not only our own lives, but those lives we touch.

Who needs the Church? You do. We all do. For everyone needs to belong to something enduring, something that will outlast the fads and fancies of the moment. Christ said that His Church will outlast them all, and that even "the gates of hell shall not prevail against it."

For continuous exposure, then, to the possibility and provision of salvation through Christ; for fellowship that enriches and ennobles; for redemptive activity that makes for better lives and a better world; for an institution which challenges us, when life matters most, to give the best that we have to the best that we know—we *all* need the Church.

What Happened to the Mourners' Bench?

We have an altar **(Heb. 13:10).**

In that historic message "All Out for Souls," the late Dr. J. B. Chapman said of the early days of our church, "The mourners' bench was the only indispensable piece of furniture in our meetinghouses."

But that was true in the early days of many evangelical

churches in America. Early Methodism, for instance, from the very beginning of the nineteenth century, made effective use of the mourners' bench—an altar of prayer. It was a place at the front of the sanctuary or auditorium or brush arbor where convicted sinners, and Christians who hungered after holiness, could kneel in penitence and supplication and faith and receive a vital, firsthand experience with God.

Other churches, also, that were warmed by the great revival fires that swept the Colonies in those early days made wide and effective use of the mourners' bench.

But what has happened? Where is the mourners' bench today? Have we outgrown the need of it? Has our space-age sophistication or our psuedo intellectualism finally made the mourners' bench obsolete?

I am one who definitely believes that, if the mourners' bench were ever needed, it is needed today!

There are others, of course, who share that conviction. The dean of a great cathedral, for instance, was asked by a younger preacher what he thought the solution was for wars and violence and the terrible erosion of morality today. The dean replied: "The mourners' bench."

But perhaps instead of asking, "What happened to the mourners' bench?" we should ask, "What happened to the sin-decrying, God-anointed preaching that made a mourners' bench necessary and worthwhile?"

"What a task confronts the American clergy—" observes Eric Hoffer, "preaching the good news of a Saviour to people who for the most part have no real sense of sin!"

And why have they no real sense of sin? Too often it is because even the word "sin" has been thrown on the ash heap of a forgotten vocabulary. "Don't say 'sin,' we are told; it might make people squeamish—it might even make them feel guilty! So just say 'maladjustment' or 'mistake' or 'disease.'"

And so the sense of personal responsibility for drunkenness and thievery and rebellion and lying and sex perversion evaporates in the sweet talk, "He can't help it; don't blame him—it's his glands, or his heredity, or his environment."

Don't you believe it! Adam's heredity was impeccable—for he came fresh from the hand of God. His environment was perfect—he didn't live in a ghetto; he lived in a garden. But he sinned. And he sinned when he chose to disobey God. And men sin today. No matter who they are or where they live or how rich or poor they are—they sin when they choose to disobey God. And their sin still separates them from God and from each other and from their best selves. The solution is not government *relief*, but God's *redemption*. And *that* is found only in Christ.

But instead of proclaiming Jesus Christ as the Son of God and the world's only Saviour, too many talk about a harmless little divinity who had his own hang-ups but who mastered them sufficiently to say some good and noble things and finally died on a cross for his impossible dream. And so, Swinbourne's prediction has come true: there are some who "for tender minds, serve up half a Christ."

"What has happened," asks Martin Marty, "to the sovereign God, the majestic and holy God? The Lord of Hosts?" And then he answers his own question by saying, "He gets lost in all the chummy, cozy, soft, sweet talk about 'making God relevant.'"

And what does that "sweet talk" about Jesus produce? It produces churches full of men and women who have a very hazy faith in a very vague religion. It produces professing Christians who are no different from other respectable sinners. It produces church members like the Hollywood actress who replied to a friend's surprise that she believed in astrology, "Oh, yes, . . . I believe in everything—a little bit."

But any church or preacher or religion that does nothing more than smooth the edges of the sinner, and talks about an emasculated Christ who is soft on sin, can never be used by God's Spirit as a redemptive agency to produce conviction for sin. Since there is no call to repentance, no remorse, no mourning over sins, naturally there will be no use for a mourners' bench.

After a profound experience in the use of a mourners' bench in California, Dr. Criswell, who is pastor of the First Baptist Church in Dallas, Tex., installed a mourners' bench in his own church. Now, Sunday after Sunday, people kneel at that mourners' bench, and Dr. Criswell says, "I cannot tell you how many times my hand, as I have bowed and prayed, has been covered with hot tears . . . and it is revival every Sunday."

Oh, what a revival might sweep America and the world if sin were again thundered against in the pulpits, if Christ were again proclaimed as the Son of God and man's only Lord and Savior, and if the mourners' bench were again the scene of needy, hungry men and women kneeling humbly before their God in repentance and faith—and finding a personal, vital, and glorious experience in Jesus Christ!

For the salvation of souls, for the renewal of the Church, for the survival of our nation and our world—may God hasten the day!

Discount-House Religion

For the time will come when they will not endure sound doctrine but . . . they shall turn away their ears from the truth, and shall be turned unto fables **(II Tim. 4:3-4).**

Two of the more popular phrases of the day are: "Take it easy," and, "Can you get it for me wholesale?"

Whole chains of discount houses have sprung up in response to that second question. Everyone is familiar with those giant stores with enormous stocks and spectacular advertising promotions that feature cut-rate prices.

This discount-house idea has invaded the churches until there are any number of places today where a religious shopper, looking for marked-down prices, can find cheap "grace."

Some churches cut the price by discounting doctrine, implying that it doesn't make too much difference what one believes, just so he is sincere in it.

"Salvation and redemption are disturbing to suburbia," writes Martin Marty, "for suburbanites like their gospel—unlike their martinis—diluted, and the peddlers of dilution are legion."

No wonder, then, that even professing Christians can speak in such chummy terms about the eternal God as "a livin' doll." Or can thumb toward heaven and glibly talk about "the man upstairs."

To all such bargain hunters, God is no longer an omnipotent Being, eternal in holiness; He is little more than a jolly Santa Claus, or a grandfatherly God who makes no real demands and merely chuckles over their sins. So, in effect, when they pray at all, they say, "Dear Grandfather which art in heaven . . ."

Farfetched, you say? But did you read in the *Ladies Home Journal* sometime ago of their survey of the religious views of 1,000 American women? "To sum it up," the article concluded, "it appears that most churchgoing American women have placed their faith in a grandfatherly God who grants security and comfort in return for fidelity to His dictates."

To those looking for cheap grace, churches which still insist on proclaiming Christ as the Son of God in a unique and eternal relationship seem quaint and old-fashioned and simply not "with it." The word, I believe, which is used to cover this antiquated theology of the deity of Jesus Christ is "irrelevant." Heresy they don't mind—just so it's "relevant."

And to all those who look for doctrine at discount prices, any mention of the Cross is crude. Oh, they don't mind a cross as decoration on their church, or even a gold cross to wear as jewelry. But a cross with *blood* on it—that is a shock to their sophisticated sensibilities. So they shop around for a bloodless religion, a crossless creed, a humanized Christ, and a grandfatherly God who is soft on sin.

But another way to peddle a discount-house religion is to cut the price of standards of Christian conduct until the church becomes just another dispenser of situational ethics and the new morality—which is to say: Do what you want, when you want, to whom you want, and wherever you want. If it makes you feel good, go ahead and do your thing; God won't mind.

No wonder that men like C. Wright Mills feel compelled to write such articles as "A Pagan Sermon to the Christian Clergy." In this article which appeared in the *Nation,* he says, "As a social and as a personal force, religion has become a dependent variable. It does not originate; it reacts. It does not denounce; it adapts. It does not set forth new models of conduct and sensibility; it imitates. Its rhetoric is without deep appeal; the worship it organizes is without piety."

Confronted with such a marked-down religion, men like A. W. Tozer warn that, "if the church of the second half of this century is to recover from the injuries she suffered in the first half, there must be a new-type preacher, the old prophet type who stands in flat contradiction to everything our smirking, smooth civilization stands for."

And on this broadcast, from week to week, we are trying our best to be that type of preacher—to proclaim a gospel that saves to the uttermost, but that demands repentance and surrender and faith. It will take that kind of gospel if God is to do His mighty works in the hearts of men and in the affairs of our nation and in the conflicts in our society.

So to all the bargain hunters, I say: "Repent ye, and believe the gospel" . . . for, "except ye repent, ye shall all likewise perish." . . . "Turn ye . . . for why will ye die?"

To all those looking for cheap grace, I say: We preach "Christ, and him crucified." . . . For "without shedding of blood [there] is no remission" of sins . . . and although "the preaching of the cross is to them that perish foolishness . . . unto us which are saved it is the power of God." . . . "For the wages of sin is death; but the gift of God is eternal life through Jesus Christ our Lord."

We do not say on this broadcast, as was the slogan of one church: "We try not to offend anybody." If you are living in sin, you *need* to feel dirty and sinful and needy and lost—otherwise you will never be willing to pay the price to be found, to be saved, to be cleaned up.

But if you are weary with shopping for discount prices, if cheap grace has proved inadequate and disappointing, and if you have become disillusioned and disgusted with a faith that hasn't cost you anything . . . I bring you good news! Look to Christ! He died for you. And the grace He died to provide is not cheap. There was no cut-rate price at Calvary. But the salvation He bought for you there will be adequate for your every need and satisfying to your deepest hunger. And when you become a recipient of His forgiving and cleansing grace, you will say, with thousands of others, that it is worth whatever price you have to pay to accept it.

Just How Great Is Our Society?

Thou sayest, I am rich, and increased with goods, and have need of nothing; and knowest not that thou art wretched, and miserable, and poor, and blind, and naked **(Rev. 3:17).**

Who hasn't heard of the "Great Society"? Or who hasn't been told, "You've never had it so good"? Meaning we have fatter paychecks, shinier cars, fancier clothes, longer vacations, color television, and split-level homes.

But do these things make a society *great?* Or a life *good?*

How great is a society that is swamped in a sea of sin and sex, of pornography and perversion and payola—while some of its psycholgists and preachers ridicule the idea of sin and, like pouring perfume over garbage, try to smother its stench with fancy words? But history's voice is clear: *Any* society that is obsessed with sex is a sick, decaying, degenerate society. And God has never put up for long with the smell of smut and decaying morals from *any* society—and He won't from ours.

How great is a society whose cities are aflame with riots and carnage, its stores looted, and its streets littered with broken glass and bleeding bodies? Can a society be called "great" when decent citizens, bewildered and humiliated by sit-ins and squat-downs and march-outs, must retreat behind barred doors while the streets fill with shouting, cursing, hating mobs. What kind of society is it when policemen are cursed and beaten and spat upon by a generation that despises all authority?

Just how great is a society whose music is a raucous medley of sound and fury, signifying nothing—except the inner confusion and utter chaos of an a-go-go age trying to make up in volume what it lacks in value, with sounds and beats to which the sophisticates of the "in" groups dance and gyrate in jerky spasms like persons in seizure or cannibals in fertility rites?

Just how great is a society that builds shrines to its entertainers, paying one of its clowns more for one motion picture than it pays its president for seven years of leadership in the highest office in the world? How great is a society that bows down to singers who can't sing and actors who can't act and yet make the blasphemous claim that they are more popular than Jesus Christ, or to other so-called "stars" who live by barnyard morals? May God forgive us for laughing at their jokes and humming their tunes and stuffing their pockets and falling at their feet—while they cynically and leeringly preside over the liquidation of our traditional values!

How great is a society in which, though church rolls keep filling up, church attendance keeps falling off, and in which theologians vie with each other in mouthing "God is dead" blasphemies? What kind of society is it in which bishops grab headlines by sanctioning premarital or extramarital sex, or by ridiculing the Virgin Birth or the deity of Christ, or by making fun of the redemptive power of that Blood spilled on Calvary's cross?

Just how great is a society when it is illegal for little boys and girls to say a prayer in a public school classroom; where it is lawful to speak of the lust and greed and Satanic influences that shaped a Hitler, but unlawful to even speak of the love and devotion and sacrifice that shaped an Apostle Paul? How great, really, is a society in which the largest university in the land can be defied and humiliated by a bunch of dirty, degenerate, bearded beatniks, along with their sympathizers among the students and on the faculty?

When you hear people say again, "You've never had it

so good," remind them, will you, that God said, "Thou sayest, I am rich, and increased with goods, and have need of nothing; and knowest not that thou art wretched, and miserable, and poor, and blind, and naked" (Rev. 3:17).

It is not higher wages, or shinier cars, or bigger houses, or color television, or wall-to-wall carpeting; it is not money, or missiles, or machines; it is not legislation, or government handouts, that make a society great. God says that it is "*righteousness* [that] exalteth a nation: but [that] sin is a reproach to any people" (Prov. 14:34).

Somebody needs to stand up and proclaim in this space age that Calvary is still more important than Cape Kennedy, that the quantity of our things is not nearly as important as the quality of our lives, that the conquering of outer space is not nearly as urgent as the mastery of the inner spaces of our souls. Someone needs to sound the warning that we will either give up our trinkets and our tinsel and our trivia and fall on our knees before God and repent of our sins, our lust, our greed, our lawlessness, our rebellions—or God will once again, as He has done many times through history, bring His judgments upon us. We cannot defy His authority, and repudiate His claims, and reject His love, without suffering the consequences.

Toynbee, the historian, reminds us that since the birth of Christ there have been 21 civilizations, and of that number 16 have died, not from external pressures, but because of collapse and decay within. Since other societies have collapsed when they became obsessed with the secular and the sensual, why do we think we can escape? We are not God's pet.

The hour is late and the darkness gathers. The only light that breaks over a darkened world is the light and power and promise of the gospel—the gospel that is still "the power of God unto salvation to every one that believeth."

Let us quit singing, in pride and conceit, "How great

we are!" but rather let us get on our knees and repent and get right with God. Then, as members of the society of the redeemed—which is the only "great society" this world will ever know—we can begin singing, in awe and reverence, "How great Thou art!"

When Can We Expect Peace?

***There is no peace, saith my God, to the wicked* (Isa. 57:21).**

In the Palace of Versailles, just outside of Paris, France, there is a table which has a rather strange and tragic historical significance. For on that table, in 1919, was signed the Treaty of Versailles, legally ending the first World War.

Little did those world leaders know, as they signed that treaty, that in a few short years that very document would be called a "scrap of paper" and the world would be plunged into the horrors of another World War—to be followed by the turmoil and bloodshed of Korea and the Congo and Vietnam.

As I looked at that table one afternoon, it seemed to me to be a symbol of man's tragic failure in his search for peace. Presidents and premiers and prime ministers have often held high the hope and promise of peace, and they are still doing it; but while they cry, "Peace, peace," the conflicts continue. Minds are still torn by tensions, and souls are still tyrannized by sin.

How many more wars must we fight, how many more billions of dollars must we spend on guns and bombs, how many more thousands of young men must die, before we wake up to the fact that God meant exactly what He said when He spoke through Isaiah saying, "There is no peace . . . to the wicked"? It is those therefore who are engaged in the war against sin, sincerely trying to get men and women right with God, who are in the forefront of the cause of bringing peace to this world. They are the original "Peace Corps." For only as men find peace with God will they ever find peace of mind, or peace of soul, or peace with each other.

"There is no peace . . . to the wicked," God says. And why? Because there can never be peace as long as there is guilt. Guilt destroys peace, for guilt tyrannizes the mind, terrorizes the emotions, and dissipates the energies of the will.

Some seem to think that Freud discovered the unconscious, but 2,600 years before Freud, Isaiah was saying, "The wicked are like the troubled sea, when it cannot rest, whose waters cast up mire and dirt" (Isa. 57:20). Oh, they have fancier words today, but a new vocabulary doesn't alter an old problem. What a picture Isaiah gives us of the unconscious mind, constantly erupting its residue of evil thoughts and imaginations and motivations and dreams and hatreds and resentments! No one can know peace with that stench rising from the sewers of the mind. No one can know peace with such evil constantly boiling and bubbling to the surface. No one can know real peace while tyrannized by his past.

One of the leading psychoanalysts in America was quoted some time ago as saying, "The objective of analysis is to free the patient from the tyranny of the past." And, oh, how the past can tyrannize and terrorize and paralyze until life is drained of meaning, of joy, and of peace!

A young wife confesses that she has known no peace for eight years because of her infidelities while her husband was away in the armed services. Guilt is a terrible tyranny.

A woman writes an insurance company and confesses that 17 years ago she set fire to a house to collect insurance, and for 17 years she has suffered torment of conscience until, as she said, "I can't take it anymore."

A man walks into the police station and confesses that he is guilty of embezzlement, and although he had the thefts well covered, he has been tormented by fear that he would be found out. Guilt is a terrible tyranny.

Some, of course, try to drown out the cries of that tyranny with liquor, or with sex, or by such hectic and feverish activity that they won't have time to think. Others try to bribe that tyranny with money given to charitable causes. But no amount of money can buy off that guilt. Money can buy many things—big cars, fine houses, expensive clothes, fabulous vacations—but no amount of money can buy peace.

What shall it profit a man if he gains the whole world, if his soul is in turmoil? What shall it profit a woman if she attains stardom in the world of movies, but is driven to suicide? One such actress left a note saying, "I'm sorry to do this, but it's the only way out."

The only way out? No. There is another way, and that way leads to a Cross where you can confess your sins and admit that you cannot break the clutches of that tyranny of guilt that hounds you and tears you to pieces, that you cannot break the chains of evil habit and sinful practice. Kneel at the foot of that Cross—will you?—and trust Christ to break those chains, to release you from that tyranny, to make you a new creature. You can be not only freed *from* the past but freed *for* a new life, on a new level, with a new purpose and a new destiny.

That is the good news I bring you. God's love in Christ will melt those chains, will dissolve those shackles, will emancipate you from the tyranny of the past, and will give you peace. And He will do it now, if you will repent and believe.

So to a world desperately searching for peace, God says, "There is no peace . . . to the wicked"—no peace in this life, in death, at the judgment, or in that eternity of separation from God. *That* is God's word. But this is also God's word: "Him that cometh unto me I will in no wise cast out." "My peace I give unto you; not as the world giveth." "These things I have spoken unto you," says Jesus, "that in me ye might have peace."

You can't find that kind of peace at the United Nations. You can't find that kind of peace in the halls of Congress or in the Kremlin or in any parliament. You can't find that kind of peace in a bank vault, or on a psychiatrist's couch.

But you can find that kind of peace at the foot of the Cross. There you, even you, no matter how troubled by sin, no matter how tyrannized by guilt, can begin to sing,

There's a deep settled peace in my soul;
There's a deep settled peace in my soul.
Tho' the billows of sin near me roll,
He abides; Christ abides.